UNFOLDING MAGIK

Learning to channel the power within

Ethean Soule
Rainbow Medium

Published in Australia by Sid Harta Publishers Pty Ltd,
ACN: 007 030 051
23 Stirling Crescent, Glen Waverley, Victoria 3150, Australia
Telephone: +61 3 9560 9920, Facsimile: +61 3 9545 1742
E-mail: author@sidharta.com.au

First published in Australia 2009
This edition published May 2009
Copyright ©Rogerson, Ethean Soule 2009
Cover design, typesetting: Chameleon Print Design

The right of Ethean Soule Rogerson to be identified as the Author of the Work has been asserted in accordance with the Copyright, Designs and Patents Act 1988.

Email:
ethean@vibrationaltherapiez.com
website:
www.vibrationaltherapiez.com

The information in this book is based on the author's personal experiences and opinions. The publisher specifically disclaims responsibility for any adverse consequences which may result from use of the information contained herein.

All rights reserved. No part of this publication may be reproduced, stored in a retrieval system, or transmitted, in any form or by any means without the prior written permission of the publisher, nor be otherwise circulated in any form of binding or cover other than that in which it is published and without a similar condition being imposed on the subsequent purchaser.

Rogerson, Ethean Soule
Unfolding Magik
ISBN: 1-921362-31-6
EAN13: 978-1-921362-31-6
pp288

About the author

Where do you start your spiritual journey? How do you know when you are picking up the qualifications for a career you never applied for? The secret is simply that you are the only candidate capable of stepping into your truth; how you get there, and which road you take, depend on what you identify with and which identities, if any, you are willing to let go of.

I was lucky to have my perception change at an early stage in my childhood development, experiencing my first awakening at the age of seven. From then on, I could see the world in a different light; people around me hadn't changed, but somehow I had and could now see with much more depth and emotion. So, what does a child do with this information? Seek others with a similar sense of knowing. I can't explain how I found others like myself, but I never questioned where I was directed, and couldn't have imagined that, by the age of ten, I would already be in tune with the natural forces around me. The most surprising of these was the "I-am" presence, although I only see this now as I look back.

This left me with a spiritual hunger, and I did not experience another peak until the age of fourteen, when I self-initiated into witchcraft, feeling whole for the first time in seven years. By the age of sixteen, I had received both my Reiki I and II attunements, and soon afterwards was invited to work at my first spiritual festival in Melbourne. Within a year I had made a connection to the Violet Flame. I went on to receive my masters in reiki and seichim when I was twenty, spending most of my time channelling information in order to strengthen my gifts.

Taking a break from my life in Melbourne, I chose to live in Port Douglas for the next few years, where I worked in a natural therapy centre as a reiki and spell consultant. Turning twenty-five, I decided to throw myself into the deep end, all or nothing, and test my psychic ability by doing an intensive psychic workshop, completing my PRV I in remote viewing. After opening Vibrational Therapiez, I started working the spiritual festivals in Brisbane.

I have worked closely with many spiritual orders: Tao, Spiritualist Church, Pagan Alliance and the Temple of Set, to name a few. You will find on your journey that you will take their essence and continue along your path, building on your truths.

I have been working with true magik for over twelve years and with reiki and seichim for nine years, on top of my extensive background in spiritualism and metaphysics. In conjunction with other light workers, and through Vibrational Therapiez, I seek to guide and support my clients through their personal experiences, giving them a unique teaching which I bring from my own spiritual journey.

I would like to say that I have a rigorous meditation regime, but once a day seems to best suit my lifestyle. I enjoy being out in nature, especially around tall trees, which reminds me to stay firmly grounded, and of course the beach, the sun being a major part of the connection to all that is. Working closely with the archetypes of ancient Egypt, I choose to anchor various types of energies through the grace of magik. Don't get caught up in concepts of worship, as everything is energy, and the only limitations we have are what we place on ourselves. I hope you have fun with all your endeavours, and don't take yourself too seriously. Blessed be.

In memory of ...
a single red feather!

Dedicated to ...

those who have enabled me and encouraged me to grow spiritually ...
Kylie and Melissa

Dedication

I sail along within a little dream of you
The current flowing steady and slow
Swirls of ocean blue and forest green pass me by
Painting the world that now I can be seen in.
I dip my hands in the tranquil waters
Of the deep blue ocean to quench my thirst
And wash my sun-beaten face
Slipping overboard without a warning
Into the cool summer water headfirst without a trace.
My body tingles all over from head to toe
As the cool water rushes past
I dive deeper into the vast ocean.
Sailing further across the ocean bed
Awaking from a dream of you
Now I know that you dream of me too.
Sitting by my porch at night
I still feel the presence of you
In the cold night air or the chill from the pouring rain.
Which reminds me of a little dream of you
Where I sailed upon your ocean
And you surrounded me with your love
A dream we shared together each night that I dream.

Acknowledgements

Following the path of a channel has been an interesting journey. There is no formal training for the knowing; all you have is the spiritual flame that ignites within you as you sit in silence. It sounds very simple when I put it like that, doesn't it? But the influx can be overwhelming at times, leaving you burnt up instead of tuned in, unable to receive.

A piece of advice I will share is to follow the guidance you receive wherever you are led, no matter how ridiculous it may seem at the time, as it may surprise you! The defining moments in my journey, the greatest spiritual lessons I have received, have been sparked not by elders, gurus or masters, but by simple gestures, the actions of someone who would otherwise raise their eyebrows at a phenomenon such as this.

I send my appreciation to the following people, who have had strong influence on my development even though they are not directly involved in this field: Kylie A., for consistently testing my abilities and pushing me to rise to each new challenge; Kathy D., for keeping me focused on my strengths and believing in my vision; Mark P., for encouraging me to write this book and express what was burning inside me; Nana M., for keeping me grounded and demonstrating how much people can transform when they let go and allow themselves to be awakened; Reuben M., for teaching me the value of humility and wisdom in all my endeavours; Luke D., for showing me my capabilities and steering me to my truth; and Judy L., for allowing me to see the path I now lead.

It can be amazing when you meet people who are not at the same level of understanding but still have a dramatic impact on your experience. This might be by giving you the answer to a question you put out to spirit, by questioning your position on faith and encouraging you to succeed, or by allowing you to see your strengths as you awaken them. We are all learning truths from each other, so make sure you pay attention: just because someone is not a spiritual teacher, this does not mean they do not have a message for you that will help you to grow.

My development has been an experience I have shared with some very beautiful souls, none of whom were what you would call a teacher, but nonetheless I have taken a great deal of wisdom from them. I express my gratitude to just a few: Melissa C. (Silver Wolf), for starting this journey with me and giving me a forum where I could grow; and Corrine C. (Cirro), for giving me the encouragement I needed to finish this book and the understanding that there are no weaknesses, only challenges we need to focus on.

These teachings come from many hours spent channelling after school. Yes, that is where it all began many years ago; I would come home, go straight to my bedroom and tune in. This was normal for me, and I didn't feel whole until I was true to myself and sat in silence ... although it was never silent for long. I was a difficult pupil for my spirit guides to train; like many of us, my desire for them to "prove it" kept coming to mind. As you'll find out, be careful with what you put out there, because here I am now, but I never would have thought I'd be working with spirit.

I thank those spiritual teachers who came in and out of my life to help me awaken to my truth: Dorothy G., not for attuning me to reiki but for giving me the opportunity to learn how to see and feel energy; Patricia G., for taking me through my reiki and seichim mastery and seeing the magik that runs through me; Simone T., for seeing who I am and helping me believe in myself; and Jason M., for encouraging me to step in my truth, enabling me to really see who I am and allow the die-offs to come naturally.

    Everyone's journey is different and there are many roads on the path. What makes it a little easier is not being too hard on yourself, and just allowing things to be. Surrender can be the biggest challenge you face; if so, then things are not as they seem. I will finish with the advice to walk humbly with a compassionate heart and an open mind.

Contents

Part I	**In the beginning...**		**1**
Chapter 1	Introduction		3
Chapter 2	The art of worship		7
	Triple Goddess		8
	Deities of the world		10
	Universal lore		13
	The angelic realm		15
	Magikal gate		20
	Freeing souls		21
Chapter 3	Erecting a temple		25
	Moon phases		26
	Casting a circle		29
	The altar		32
	Tool box		33
	Magikal names		40
	Self-initiation		42
Part II	**What comes naturally...**		**45**
Chapter 4	Awakening the third eye		47
	Cradled discs		52
	Basic meditation		55
	Inducing a trance		57
Chapter 5	Natural power		63
	Scrying		71
	Cord magik		73
	Broom magik		74
	Tarot magik		77
	Elemental magik		80

Chapter 6	Life force	87
	Inside spells	88
	Energy types	89
	The aura	93
	The chakras	96
Chapter 7	Power of healing	99
	The art of channelling	101
	Colour therapy	108
Part III	**Putting magik into practice**	**119**
Chapter 8	Ritual craft	121
Chapter 9	Psychic protection	125
Chapter 10	True magik	141
Chapter 11	Empowerment	175
Part IV	**The broom closet**	**187**
Chapter 12	Book of shadows	189
Chapter 13	Psychic art gallery	223
Part V	**Final notes**	**229**
	Awakening or psychosis?	231
	Afterword	239
Appendices		241
Appendix A	Magikal numbers	241
Appendix B	Colours	242
Appendix C	Crystals	243
Appendix D	Aromatherapy oils	244
Appendix E	Spell register	245
Occult glossary		259

Part I

In the beginning

Chapter 1

Introduction

This book is about all that exists. It delves into the heart of several beliefs, representing an entire life's work rolled into one final chapter in which chaos, love and pain all come together. Being a part of the old religions has enriched my life immensely. Despite the fact that they all speak of an entity, a godly force that governs our lives, I wouldn't part with any of them. Following only one faith wasn't enough to satisfy my own beliefs! I have been working with magik for over twelve years now, and also practising spiritualism for nine years, in addition to my experiences within the occult. What does that make me – a witch, a pagan, a spiritualist or a magician? Not at all. We do not need to be a part of any religion, cult or sect. Our faith, our own beliefs, will guide us towards what our spirit longs for. We can agree with the practices of witchcraft but also value the key principles of spiritualism, that is ok too. God, or Goddess if you prefer, has many faces and your prayers will be answered. All you need is belief, not only in the role of the divine but, most importantly, belief in yourself. Trusting in the divine and in yourself illuminates the connection between the worlds and creates a bridge of love and light which, my friend, is magik in itself. This book is titled *Unfolding magik – learning to channel the power within* because that is what magik is, in its purest form.

I am a spirit and always will be although I follow my own heart and a set of beliefs that I have adapted from many faiths as we know them. To give you an overview, I have a deep respect for the god energies of Ancient Egypt; they are present in my everyday life just as they were for those back in ancient times. I also carry with me belief in the ministry of angels and the art of reiki (universal healing). Neither belongs to a particular religion, but they are evident in spiritualism and the study of vibrational therapy. With my unorthodox and unique method of ritual construction, the intent is to extend your magikal horizon, opening a gateway to true magik. You need not my words but the message contained within them. The means to your end starts from trusting your intuition and developing further from that train of thought. It is important to connect everything you see, feel and hear on all planes of existence throughout your daily routine. Whether you're working or at leisure, you will see how the environment, the people, their thoughts and energy at play, all come together to create what has been variously called coincidence, light, euphoria and ecstasy. This is a measure that has been taken by spirit on your behalf to aid in your evolution, your enlightenment as part of this divine consciousness, spiritual force that you are. In turn this can be seen as the knowing ... true magik!

We masters of magik know that this force is powerful and acknowledge its greatness. With respect, we must live within it as intended, altering not just the energy that surrounds but ourselves and the people within our reach. I once had a wise question put to me during the completion of my first manuscript. It was: "If you achieved all your desires, and through magik you attained all wisdom, what then?" In answer, all I said was that, no matter how far I travel with magik, whatever sights I may envision, I will still have more to learn. There will always be further lessons. I first threw away childish things when I began to master a way to channel this, the knowing, the way it has always been. Magik allows you to grow and develop your evolutionary process. Listen to what your heart tells you and remove the emotions of doubt and disbelief. In this book I give you the tools needed in order to proceed and, most importantly, the knowledge you gain within these pages will enable you to understand and follow the path that lies before you.

> *When you peer upon your collection of spells and come to realise that they are not yours, then put away such childish things, for they are mere training wheels of what is now to come.*

If I were to ask you to pick up a broomstick, would you start sweeping or would you ride beside me? Are you lost? Then I'm afraid this book isn't for you. Some experience, a background in the study of metaphysics, is necessary for you to continue, although a dedicated novice may endeavour to achieve success. The magikal lessons, first of all, are designed to create understanding of the basics, to ensure we're on the same page. Thereafter, it's up to you. Rely on your own potential and channel what you need, inspire yourself to write, and by doing these things create the spells and rituals best suited for you. Allow yourself to be taken on a spiritual journey through the truth behind the magik of faith. You don't need a temple to commune with God, or a set of rules to live by in order to ascend to the afterlife, nor do you have to believe in the same god that others believe in. Your faith is just that – yours!

Chapter 2

The art of worship

Wherever you find faith, not far behind is a force that guides it. This is a divine being, an unknown entity that embodies the universal secrets and power upon which your beliefs are structured. It is in the act of worship and prayer that we seek to understand this underlying force governing our lives. If we are to commune with and grow to understand the basic nature of this higher power naturally, the next step is to create representations of its divine nature which we can comprehend. Looking back into religious history, the people of past times sought to worship deities that would enrich their lives. An example of this is in the early representation of the Wiccan horned god, which clearly illustrates his nature as a hunting god. He is depicted as half-man, half-beast, with horns extending from his forehead, to show that his influence also governs the animal kingdom. From this representation we can see that he is a god who would look after a village's herds of goats and cattle in the summer and guard its stores of grain and vegetables in the winter. As people then looked to the gods for answers, it followed that if there was a god for hunting, there must also be gods for music and dance, the sun and moon, and so on. Over time, those of the old religions came to worship the gods as two separate deities, not excluding those individual gods they built their faith upon, but incorporating them together. They are known today as the God and Goddess.

You can worship the universal power in its feminine and masculine forms. Although the presence of both the God and Goddess are equally important, the Goddess has a greater significance within several practices of witchcraft. This is evident in the Goddess' role as a principal deity. When worship of the Goddess first arose, it wasn't any easy task because She has a vast array of powers. She has been classified as Mother Earth, as the protector of women's rights, the goddess of fertility and the keeper of knowledge. Since her role as the Goddess is endless, she is best described as the Triple Goddess, with three aspects of her true nature that can be worshipped separately or as a whole.

Triple Goddess

The three faces of the Goddess describe her divine nature. Within the Maiden, Mother and Crone, three sisters bound together, lie the mysteries of the Goddess.

The Maiden
She represents the birth of inspiration and creativity. She is virgin in nature and personifies innocence and true beauty. Her youthfulness shows that She is capable of change and reversing the ageing process but She is also a seductress, and a keeper of balance and harmony within nature.

The Mother
She represents the creation of life and the teaching of those within that lifecycle of being. She embodies all aspects of motherhood and governs responsibility, loyalty, respect and self-discipline. She is the greatest side of the Goddess because, as the Mother, Her prime role is to offer guidance and unconditional love.

The Crone
She represents death, an ending of a cycle as well as reincarnation.

The nature of the Crone is sometimes unclear but we do know that She holds all secrets and is the mistress of wisdom. Her key role dwells in the extension of power and knowledge. The Crone will unlock psychic gateways and protect you at any cost. She is a great magikal ally!

When it comes to worshipping the God and Goddess, you may wish to leave the titles as they are, but bestowing names upon them will enhance your connection with them. Some choose to use the names of ancient gods such as Pan, a Greek god who resembles the Wiccan horned god, and Diana, a Roman goddess who demonstrates the same qualities as the Goddess we know and love. As with anything you practice, the belief behind your techniques is what sets you aside from others. Although you must follow the key principles behind your craft, adding to these your own set of beliefs will enable you to achieve a far greater level of magikal expertise, instead of just reading from texts without truly delving into your magikal potential.

Within my craft I incorporate the Triple Goddess into my daily routine except that, when I perform a ritual, instead of the Crone I invoke Hecate, the warrior-goddess. She is usually feared because of her dark tendencies, but I have formed a strong relationship with this goddess and only use the force of her power, not the evil that may lie within. The primary Goddess I worship has all the properties of the Wiccan Goddess. Her name is Ishtar, the Babylon creator-goddess. As for the God, I use the name of the god of thunder, Thor. He is often depicted as a Norse god, but has many parallels: he is known as Jupiter in Rome and Zeus in Greece. We can choose the name of a god and then connect to them through a different origin, but it is the same presence; I find that I connect to Thor's energy more strongly this way. The most important goal is to achieve a genuine connection and, if you cannot link with a particular god, then try connecting with one of their counterparts.

I work from the ancient Egyptian teaching that names hold great power. When I perform magik I use the names of the ancient Egyptian gods Anubis, Thoth, Osiris, Horus, Bast and so on, because of my personal connection with these energies. Belief in ancient gods can be as powerful now as it was in the past, or even greater. It depends on the strength of your faith in them. Learn all you can before you commit to a name or god you wish to worship, or an energy you wish to work with, and you will make the right decision. Then, when it comes to invoking the God and Goddess, you will do this with conviction and absolute faith.

To help you find the God and Goddess that are right for you, I have included a list of popular and less wellknown gods worshipped around the world. Read through this list and discover the many faces of our blessed Lord and Lady; see how, although the archetypes are different, their divine traits still shine through, and you may discover a deity that relates closely to your spiritual needs.

Deities of the world

Asia

Apna-Apha	dual deity, Apna meaning "mother earth," Apha "father earth"
Balin	creator god of life, the soul
Kagutsuchi	god of fire
Kuan Shen Ren	god of rain
Kuan Yin	goddess of mercy
Petali	goddess of rebirth, death
Sihar	god of the four winds
Ta-iti	god of morning
Ts'ai Shen	god of wealth
Ye rje	god of being

Babylon

Era	god of disease, plague
Ensum	dual deity of the Moon, tides and time
Kittu	goddess of justice
Tiamat	goddess of the sea, giving birth to both serpent and dragon
Tillili	Earth god
Tutu	god of true magik
Uggae	god of rebirth, death
Zikun	queen of the gods

Greece

Aphrodite	goddess of love
Helios	god of light, visions
Hera	queen of the gods
Hermes	god of winds, messenger
Jove	god of the universe, justice, knowledge
Ker	god of rebirth, death
Kesar	weather god
Pegaia	goddess of healing
Phantasos	god of dreams
Zeus	king of the gods, the universe

India

Agastya	god of teaching
Ahkushta	dual deity of birth
Ankamma/Hardahin	goddess of disease
Begawati	goddess of black magik
Dhatr	creator god of the universe
Ganesh	elephant god, remover of obstacles
Gauri	god of abundance
Indra	god of cursing/spirits that aid sight, visions

Matabai	dark goddess, fury and strength
Rati	goddess of desire
Sedi	Earth goddess
Shiva	dual deity of creation and destruction
Songkam	dark god, death and evil spirits

Maya

Acral Chel	Moon goddess
Beeze	god of prosperity
Citzel	god of rebirth, death
Itzamma	god of wisdom
Quicxic	god of the afterlife

Sudan

Aeek	god of agriculture
Acek	Earth god
Cul	god of wind, dreams
Nialic	creator goddess of life

Other deities

Albina (Italy)	goddess of light, protection
Amun (Eygpt)	king of the gods, the universe
Banshees (Ireland)	gods of magik, spirits of friendship
Eita (Italy)	god of the afterlife, the dead
Oshala (Brazil)	creator god
Raven (N America)	fire god, trickery and shape-shifting
Tepeyollotli (Aztec)	creator god
Viracocha (Inca)	supreme creator god

Universal lore

While harnessing magik, we acknowledge a power far greater than our own. This intelligence gives us a unique responsibility to enjoy a harmonious existence with nature, which is why we abide by a hidden set of laws that govern such power. In witchcraft you find these laws within the Wiccan rede "Ain't it harm none, do what thou wilt" and in the karmic axiom "What you send out returns threefold." These are both brief and straight to the point. Only practise magik that will not harm you or another person. The laws of that great power can be classified into five groups: secrecy, harmony, worship, power and coven dynamics – although each coven has its own laws, there are laws that govern all, not only those within an individual coven.

Secrecy

Witchcraft is like a book of shadows. Within its pages this book contains sacred rituals and magikal practices, your beliefs and your life's work. Keep something so valuable close to your heart where it belongs. Your faith is an extension of yourself and you would not give any part of it away. Even when you are casting a spell or working magik, the key principle is secrecy between those who perform it. If you were to perform a spell while at the same time unveiling the desired outcome, that could change the course of the spell. All thoughts and actions other than those working solely on what is to be manifested may inadvertently influence a spell's success. I call this time the manifestation period because, as your focus starts to form, it is vital that your emotions and energy are used constructively. In a coven there will undoubtedly be a set of rules that you must abide by, but one in particular is the secrecy of its members.

Harmony

In everyday life it is unwise to consume alcohol and drugs, and the same goes for the practice of witchcraft. When working magik you need to have complete control, and it is prohibited to take anything that could result in you losing control. It is our way to respect the rituals and ideas of others, as in this we can learn and evolve as one. But we do not accept the notion of absolute evil, nor do we have such deities within our religion. As the children of Mother Earth, we acknowledge the presence of evil within her control and choose not to harness her destructive capabilities. Witchcraft is a religion of nature. Within its practices, we strive to create a more harmonious place for ourselves and others.

Worship

The God and Goddess are always present; we must show gratitude for all they have given us and for their help with what we wish to achieve. Witchcraft is a blessing upon all those who follow the path of light. Not everyone can be a witch, but it can inspire greatness within us: in that lies the true nature of a witch. Strive each day to strengthen your faith through dedications to the God and Goddess. When performing a ritual, always invite Them to attend as you work your magik. Building a relationship with any entity you invoke regularly will extend your magikal capabilities.

Power

Never use magik for prideful gain because, even if you obtained your desires, this would result only in pain and suffering. True magik is no illusion, nor is it a trick performed by a sideshow magician. Magik will not work in order for you to amuse your ego or impress another. It is not to be sold for services or money, as greed would soon take control. Power is a sacred gift bestowed upon us and should never be practised with the intent to harm or control another. This would take away your right to direct your own life by the correct use of that power.

Coven dynamics

Witchcraft is a very diverse religion and leaves no room for discrimination; all that is asked of you is that you look after yourself and the wellbeing of others. Teach what you know from the heart with no prideful glory. Share your knowledge with everyone who truly wishes to learn the mysteries of the God and Goddess, and also learn from those you teach. A coven should always work towards becoming one mind and one body. This will enchant the gathering and heighten the experience.

It is not for me to dictate what laws you choose to abide by or what kind of faith you decide to follow. All I can do is tell you about what I have come to know as my truths and let you make the final choice. I have included here the fundamental principles that are practised by members of the spiritualist church. I find part of my beliefs stemming from the spiritual faith. As you will see, many if not all of these principles relate in some way to those laws we abide by in Wicca.

Principles of spiritualism

- the fatherhood of man
- the brotherhood of mankind
- the communion of spirits and the ministry of angels
- the continuous existence of the human soul
- personal responsibility
- compensation and retribution for all good and evil deeds done on Earth
- eternal progress open to every human soul.

The angelic realm

There are many interpretations of angels, there characteristics, the number of angels in existence, whether or not they are winged, whether or not they serve our or a higher purpose. I have searched for answers and, like many of you, have found conflicting responses. What one must first see is that although the terms "angel" and "spirit" may seem to refer to the same entities, their true meanings are very much separated from one another.

Angels are messengers. They take the form of light, their wings represent their power, and their love, the closeness they have with God and the light that surrounds them and penetrates our souls. Angels mediate between the realm of space and time, cause and effect, and that place we call the celestial realm. They transmit the prayers of humanity and the will of God, and are a necessary medium that in its purest form can be described as a link, a higher power, the voice of God.

Spirits are celestial bodies. They take the form of thoughts and actions; very rarely do they appear in human form, but come as dreams, visions, and as direction and guidance. We cannot become angels, for they are created by God to work on behalf of humanity. Spirits, on the other hand, do not mediate between Man and his creator, but work beside us to aid in their own evolution as well as the evolution of mankind itself.

They teach, guide, heal and give us the inspiration, even the push we need to make decisions. In the earthly realm we are here to learn. Once we cross over, we become beacons of our acquired knowledge; in spirit we are able to share with those still in body, so they can evolve spiritually and we too can evolve and take a higher place in God's kingdom.

Band of angels

Do we aspire to be angels? Do we evolve to become God or divine in nature? It is thought that we are already part of God, already divine. What separates us from spirits is our bodies, and what separates spirits from angels is the angels' connection to the higher power.

Then what of these angels …
Do they all stand beside God or walk with Man?
Are there different types of angels? What are they?
To leave you with just an interpretation of an angel
Is not enough! For questions like these will still remain.
It is clear that there cannot be one angel
To work on behalf of all,
Nor can there be only one group of angels
That leaves us here at the band of angels.

Can the hidden world of angels be perceived by humans? According to the theologian Dionysius the Areopagite, it is possible. In the sixth century when the hierarchy of angels was formulated, it was described how angels are found under three distinctive bands, or levels of existence, which branch out into the nine choirs of angels that travel between Man and God.

The nine choirs of angels

I.
1. seraphim — representations of divine love
   - dispel evil
   - surround the throne of God
   - highest vibration
2. cherubim — representations of divine knowledge
   - the voice of God
   - enlighten lower-level angels
   - guardians of God's purpose
3. thrones/ophanim — representations of divine will
   - maintain harmony
   - karmic balance
   - rule over justice and mercy

II.
4. dominations/ representations of divine command
   dominions
   - oversee the duties of angels
   - manifestation of God's purpose
   - channels of mercy
5. virtues   representations of divine action
   - carry out instructions from dominations
   - spread inspiration and hope
   - chief angels of miracles on earth
6. powers/   representations of divine authority
   dynamis
   - fight against evil
   - protect divine plans
   - thought to be the first angels created

III.
7. principalities representations of divine guidance
   - linked to the powers
   - incorporate a balance of good and evil
   - oversee actions of Earth nations/humanity
8. archangels representations of divine soldiers
   - carriers of divine secrets
   - chief angels/messengers of God
   - fallen angels
9. angels   representations of divine messages
   - Mankind's connection to God
   - deliver the prayers of humanity
   - work closely with other choirs – on behalf of Man and God

Archangels

Archangels represent the four corners of the world and together symbolise God's presence, the universal power. Although they are representations of the elemental forces in nature, do not mistake them for the elementals. In Wicca, elementals are classed as spirits, which suggests that they have their own karmic evolution, although in spiritualism this can be disputed. They are seen as one and the same, part of and not separate from evolution. Below I give you a list of both the known archangels and those who could be described as fallen, the angels who go against God's purpose, the entities who are willing to tell God's secrets, which has resulted in their being expelled from His kingdom. Always remember: If there are nine angels of light on one side, there are sure to be nine equally strong angels on the other.

Archangels	Fallen angels
Uriel	Ariel
Raguel	Azael
Seraqael	Samael
Anael	Zerachiel
Haniel	Loci
Gabriel	Sariel
Michael	Azazel
Raphael	Lucifer
Auriel	Ramiel

The angel Azael has been known to be summoned in ceremonial magik, for he guards hidden treasures. Ramiel, on the other hand, is thought to aid in the interpretation of visions. There will always be diverse views about the nature of angels, archangels and fallen angels, the number of angels and which ones have fallen. I give you this as a guide, not as fact. Who can truly say? Those we speak of are celestial in nature. I have been granted my knowledge through spirit and life experiences. In time, learn to trust the messages that the angels bring, as they only send us what will aid in our evolution.

Magikal gate – opening a door to spirit

With the temple door closed, draw a doorway with either your magik (dominant) hand or atheme, knowing that spirits can only travel in and out through this gate into your temple.

Ritual to Osiris:

> Here stands a man/woman, divine in nature.
> He/she knows all, is all. He whom is creator, father,
> lord of the universe. I kneel to thee, Osiris,
> oh king of the gods, lord of the dead.
> To which I know your name, thy sacred nature.
> In that your power forever kindles in the eternal flame.
> It is he, Wennefer, who makes writing speak,
> Brings order to the west. For this command of thee,
> The power I must possess.
> With power over the west at my command, Wennefer!
> Open up a magikal gateway, to the realm of the dead.
> The key you lay in my hand.
> Standing by the gate, to me you defend.
> In this I create a gate, between worlds.
> On one side a crook and on the other a flail
> Protected by Osiris, is my temple and soul,
> From all spiritual evil.

Once you have completed the ritual to Osiris, open the temple door slightly and gaze out. You will sense spiritual activity and may be able to glimpse a spirit or two. You now hold the key to this magikal gate. Whenever you wish spirits to leave the temple, this can be done simply by slamming shut the temple door, although slamming doors will inhibit spiritual activity, and in turn close the gateway.

Freeing souls

Working with energy and the manipulation of that hidden force when performing magik will affect your life in many positive ways. But be aware that, if you apply yourself to the practice of that energy constantly, you open yourself up to other potentials which could be harmful. When using this energy on a regular basis, your soul becomes what is known as a "beacon of the light," as if it imitates the energy you are channelling. This is commonly found in the field of healing and in the growth of your psychic capabilities. In other words, when you tap into the universal energy, over time this practice will cause you to become a link, a source of this energy. You are divine in nature; thus, when you continue to channel divine energy, you become a beacon of that divine light. Because of this, you may also become a target for roaming souls, entities that are trying to find a way into the afterlife. As they search the world in an attempt to leave this plane, you as a practitioner of the universal energy are seen as a beacon of light, a light which is often mistaken for "thee light," the bridge between our world and the afterlife. This is why I believe the next technique is essential.

This meditation is a simple and effective way of directing lost entities to the light they are desperately searching for. All that you need to do is point them in the right direction and free their souls. Not every spiritual being you come in contact with is there to guide you, nor are they there for mischievous reasons. Always question them, no matter what your relationship with the entity is; whenever you sense the slightest feeling of uncertainty about them, perform this technique and the entities who are not there to guide you will leave the room.

Freeing soul meditation

For this ritual you are to cast a circle, without the aid of any tools or an altar. All that is needed is the materials you draw or create the circle with and four white candles that are to be placed at the cardinal points. Cleanse yourself with water and perfume the room with sandalwood and cedar before you begin. You are to be skyclad or clothed in a single white robe. To fast before this technique is not necessary, but will heighten the sense of purity you are to achieve. The candles within the circle are to be the only source of light. Thus the meditation must be performed at night, most importantly at a time of absolute silence. If possible, the circle is to be situated in the centre of the room. Once you are cleansed, begin by setting up the circle, then sit at its core. Clear your mind of the entities around you, for they are bound outside the circle. Maintaining the sensation of their presence, but without connecting to it, start to enter a meditative state. You will naturally begin by relaxing your entire body. As you do so, visualise yourself filling up with the brightest light. At this point try not to dwell on the entities, keeping them in the back of your mind. Once you are completely relaxed and filled with this divine light, the process of freeing their souls will begin.

At this point, maintain your breathing and visualise the energy that you have channelled flowing out from and back into the circle. As it engulfs the internal sphere of the circle, it will begin to rise above your head to form a cone. Once this has been achieved, bring your thoughts back to the entities that surround you and visualise the cone of energy rapidly leaving the circle and merging with the entities within the room. When this takes place, you are acting as an amplifier to join all the souls into the light, and at that very moment all the entities will fly towards the top of the energy cone. Simultaneously it will shoot out into the universe, spiralling like a cyclone. Within its centre, the souls are set free. They feel an overwhelming pull towards this, filled with a sense of peace and purity. Remaining in control will enable you to take from this experience the sense of love that you felt as you connected with those entities and sent them back home. Once the souls are released, the tunnel you created will dissipate. You should slowly draw the energy down and earth it while you start to ground your own energy, then wake from this meditation and close the circle.

Spiritual attunement – unlock hidden whispers of spirit

"I sit here in the darkness, it's cold, I'm alone, disconnected. Absent but that's not it, not me, not what this is. I'm a medium, a channel for you to tune into, find your truths. See the light, not as me, but as it should be. Not so dark, to feel alone anymore. To validate your grief, your love, most of all you believe … in something greater than ourselves!"

This will take you on a journey through places unknown. As a ritual within the spoken word, you will follow a path to ascend to a higher level of being. In this you will commune with those who are the "silent helpers." Begin by making a mental affirmation of the time you wish to perform the ritual. This is to let the spirit world know of your intention to have contact with them. Then, when it is time, say:

I call my spirit guides to be near.
In circle around, behind thee
Only of divine light and unconditional love
Thus of pure intent, shalt ye spirits appear before me.
I sit in silence, absent from thought.
Pure and free to believe
Readily I wait, Thy presence.
For your message I will receive.
Lift me out of my sense of depth, beyond the clouds
Though the door between worlds. Immersed in your love
Safe and sound, floating free from Thy earthly realm!
In an astral state, I now besiege.
To which I am no longer bound

The ability to communicate with Thy spirit,
To emerge in the light of the divine
Shalt this powerful gift, forever be mine
Throughout space and time!

It is important to note that, whenever you are summoning an entity, even if you believe it to be good in nature, always ask if it comes from the light. Their intent must be pure and for your benefit, in the highest love and light.

Many people make contact with spirit in their own way, through their thoughts, inner voices, through music or prayer, in writing or through the arts. The key is to explore all these techniques and find whichever one appeals to your soul. This may not be clear, or you may have many talents. Every one of us has hidden potential: it is up to the individual to open up the possibilities of not only believing but knowing!

Chapter 3

Erecting a Temple

The practice of magik should be done in a harmonious place where the energies raised and spirits evoked are contained and kept from wandering after a ritual has been performed. Known as a temple, it is the place where you cast your circles and call on the presence of the God and Goddess, a protective room of light and love devoted to all that is spiritual in nature. There must be no clutter. Have only the bare essentials required for the practice of your faith. This includes a permanent altar, a bookcase that holds your library of occult interests, a chest full of ritual tools and materials and, finally, the outline of a circle on the temple floor. This is the ideal set-up. However, if you are unable to dedicate a room solely to the purpose, creating a temple within your bedroom will work in the same manner, as long as you meet these requirements and create a harmonious environment within that room. When you decide on the room that you wish to use as a temple, you must then cleanse it on both the astral and physical levels. Since temple dedication is such a personal matter, I have included a ritual to which you can add your own style and energy; after all, it is your sacred place of worship.

**Sacred space ritual –
the creation of a magikal temple**
   I cast a circle within my room
   Forever open and never closed

May it protect me from harm!
Keep out any negativity and evil sent.
I take this incense, seal the doors and windows shut!
I cleanse the corners, the temple within
Which only love and light may thrive.
I take the holy water, to it I charged
Taking it to the four corners, I now cleanse
To the temple be sealed
Only spirits of light may enter, by choice of mine.
My will is as strong as the gods,' as is my temple
It will remain a source of divine energy
That is continuously alive
Always open, in service to me
Where only love will thrive.

Moon phases

Whether you are dedicating a circle to the worship of the God and Goddess or the practice of magik, some consideration needs to be given to the influences outside your control, in particular, the phases of the Moon. As you may be aware, the Moon plays an important role in the shifting climate, land and sea, so what role do these phases play in magik? Keeping track of which phase the Moon is currently in is important, because whether the Moon is waxing or waning will determine the type of magik you should be performing.

Waxing Moon

When the waxing Moon is present, it is the time to perform constructive magik. This is a period that represents opportunity, wealth, love, success, fertility and protection; anything that can be regarded as growth.

Waning Moon

When the waning Moon is present, it is the time to perform destructive magik. This represents a period of decline, departure, binding and extermination; anything that relates to the release of suffering.

Phases of the moon

The moon travels through a periodic cycle. It begins at the new Moon, then passes through the first quarter, then proceeds to the final phase, the full Moon, which is the first sequence of the waxing period.

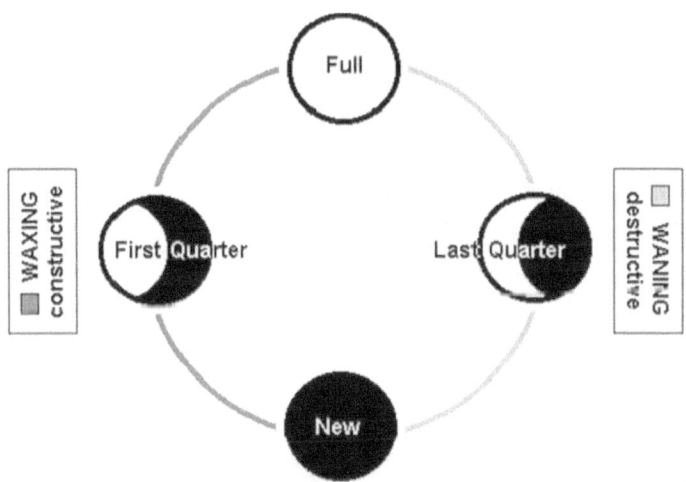

Once the Moon has reached its full Moon phase, it then follows the remaining part of the cycle by passing through the last quarter, then returning to the new Moon; this is the waning period. Once the Moon completes the cycle, it continues travelling through all four phases.

Full Moon rite

    Mistress of the darkened skies
    Lunar goddess
    Sending down your rays of light
    I thank you for watching over my life.
    Sacred lady of the universe
    Creature of the night
    Reveal again your mysterious way
    Pull once more the tides
    To the full moon, I do pray.
    In your honour I gather here tonight
    Welcoming the waxing of your power
    To let you know the source of my love
    Will never wane in the darkest hour.

New Moon rite

    I welcome the scent of change in the air
    Looking up into the night sky
    Beyond the cloud and stars
    Knowing the goddess is not far behind.
    She is in the changing seasons
    The darkened wheel of life
    Ending and beginning

All that is in her sight.
I depart from the old and greet the new
By the waning of the darkened moon
I ask the goddess to watch over me once more
As a child who has now been reborn!

Casting a circle

> I am a white witch; all the magik I perform is of the highest light. I dedicate my rituals in honour of the God and Goddess; my prayers go only to spirits of their unconditional nature, their love.

Good intentions are not always rewarded. In fact, magik and other forms of psychic research do not fall neatly into categories of good and evil, black and white. True magik, like nature, cannot be described in its real form, only in the way we direct it to influence our lives. A circle represents wholeness, a purity that cannot be penetrated, a beginning and an end, a continuous cycle. Once the circle is complete, no harm shall fall upon those in its sphere. It is a haven within which to perform a healing, cast magik or recite a simple prayer ... Imagine you are in a circle of mirrors with no way out. Now you cast your magik. The energy raised bounces off you and spins around the circle, magnifying the ritual being performed. At the same time, the energy is being directed outward so as to protect you from evil, however subtle. I will show you how to create a circle of your own, and take you step-by-step through various types of circles. A circle can be created out of stone and crystal, rope and string, candles and incense, paint and chalk and, at the extreme, blood and knives.

Traditionally a circle is nine feet in diameter, with a candle placed at each cardinal point. You need not invoke the corners or the God and Goddess. The circle that you create requires only your will to keep it intact. Start by collecting several cords, preferably of earth tones, and tie them together to form a circle of a size that fits your need. You will require enough room for an altar and maybe a healing blanket, and plenty of room to move around and perform your ritual. If you lie down, this will give you a basis for the diameter of the circle. The reason for using several cords is that, as you learn and evolve within your magikal practices, so too does your circle. Knowing this, you will be able to determine if the current size of the circle is still relevant, meaning, as need dictates. You can open up one of the ties and either add an additional cord or subtract as many cords as you require. This allows your circle to become a part of you and your spiritual growth. Once you have created a circle of cords, lay it out, not worrying too much about its circular shape, as the energy raised only needs to encircle you. Before you begin, it is important to understand the correct process of maintaining that energy: once cast, you are able to exit and enter the circle without breaking the connection.

Exiting the circle

With your dominant hand, draw a line over the east side of the circle, then draw another, two feet apart, on the right side of that line. In doing this, you have created a doorway between your circle and the outside room that hasn't resulted in the circle being closed. You have now set up two mirrored walls that allow the circle's energy to circulate continuously while you exit through the gap you have now created.

Entering the circle

It is important to remember that the circle is still cast. Before you attempt to re-enter it, to help recall the exact location of the doorway I find it easy to place something outside the circle where the doorway is located. Step through the doorway, the two-foot gap between each line previously drawn. Once in the circle, again with your dominant hand, draw a line. In this case you draw a line across the gap you created, sealing the circle shut. An additional technique to use once you have sealed the circle is to draw a pentagram in front of the doorway. This adds extra strength to the gap you have closed. Apart from exiting and entering a circle, all you need to remember about casting a circle is that you are directing energy through yourself and into the walls that make up the outside of the sphere.

Taking all this into consideration, you are now ready to cast a circle. With your circle laid upon the ground, step inside. Standing at the east, point your dominant hand down to the circle and direct the energy into it. Continue to direct the energy down into the circle as you walk around its edge, back to where you started from. The circle is now complete! Next is a brief overview of the other types of circles. It doesn't matter what materials you use to create the circle; the process remains the same.

Paint and chalk

When away from the temple, carrying a piece of chalk will act as a temporary measure to aid you, wherever you may be, in creating a circle. Paint, on the other hand, is used to create a permanent fixture: when you have dedicated a room to the practice of magik, your circle can be painted on the temple floor.

Stones and crystals

If using stones, collect the type of stone that you have around you at that particular time. Gather four stones that are roughly the same size. Place one stone at each cardinal point, using them to map out the circle's diameter. If using crystals, the same process applies. It is best to collect four clear-quartz crystals. This will help in the raising and directing of energies.

Knives

You will need four blades, each placed, as with the previous method, at each cardinal point. This should be performed outdoors, for you need to push the blades into the ground, facing outwards. Once each knife is in place, run a string around them to create the circle.

The altar

Herbs and candles are not necessary for every spell. The same applies to the altar. You won't need to use your altar every time you create your circle; it is only there to hold all the essential materials for a ritual. If the spell you to cast does not require any basic elements, then there is no harm in omitting the altar.

Where should you place the altar: towards the east, west, north or south? Finding out which element corresponds best with your nature will help you make the right decision. Like your temple, the altar is an expression of your faith, an extension of yourself and your very beliefs. Whether it is a table, a box or a plank of wood, your altar should be personalised and decorated in such a fashion that it speaks your name. Each altar requires eight basic elements in order to function correctly; adding a theme or your own personal touch to its design will bring it into harmony with the temple and, fundamentally, yourself.

The eight elements of an altar
- chalice or wine glass
- atheme/sword or wand
- salt and water dishes
- mixing bowl (heatproof)
- the book of shadows/magikal text
- God and Goddess representations (symbolic)
- 1 black and 1 white candle
- incense and burner.

The key principle behind the set-up of the altar is balance. Begin by taking your symbols of the God and Goddess and place them some distance apart, one on each side, standing them together with either a black or white candle. The four bowls (for the salt and water, the mixing bowl and the chalice) should be on one side and the atheme (sword or wand) on the other. That leaves the centre of the altar for the magikal text and the top, the space between the two symbols, is for the incense and burner.

Tool box

Primary tools
Within the practice of magik, four primary tools are required. Their significance can be seen in the tarot, as the same symbology is used throughout the minor arcana cards, commonly referred to in ancient Egypt as the book of Thoth, as he has also been referenced as a god

of magik. Separately they represent the basic elements, and together they form the Akasha. They are listed below with their counterparts:

- sword (athame)
- wand (staff)
- cup (chalice)
- shield (pentacle)

Sword (double-edged blade)

You might assume the sword's purpose is to cut, but in a physical sense it is not! Traditionally the sword or ritual knife is used for the direction of energy raised during a magikal rite or spell. The energy channelled through the practitioner can be stored within its blade by the same process by which you would charge a crystal. Known as the athame in Wicca, this is its use throughout the practice of true magik.

Wand

In many ways the wand can be used in the absence of a sword. It too can be used for the direction of energy. The wand works as a scribe, drawing the circle around you and revealing hidden spirit words; at the same time it brings a strong connection to the animal kingdom.

Cup (celestial cauldron)

Known as the chalice, you will find it used mainly in rituals. It is used to hold wine for blessings and water for scrying. The cup itself symbolises abundance or the lack of. Placing it upon your altar with water inside will increase the flow of abundance, creating a more harmonious temple.

Shield

The use of the shield is rare in Wicca, but it is as vital to your rituals as the athame. It is commonly found only in the practice of ceremonial magik, for its protective and powerful properties. A pentacle can also act as a shield, for it represents the same qualities.

Secondary tools

You will need your secondary tools when performing a ritual or casting a spell. These are what I call magikal aids because, when you need to create a potion, cleanse or summon natural energies, all that is required can be found on the list of tools below.

- cauldron (transformation)
- incense (purify/invoke)
- bell (energy vibrations)
- broom (banish/protect)
- jewellery (empowerment)

Cauldron

This is the ultimate tool for a witch, a vessel that embodies all aspects of the Goddess. Symbolising fertility and the creation of magik, the cauldron corresponds to the element of water, the pouring in of knowledge and the stirring of one's fate.

Incense

The method behind the use of incense is simply this: to summon, banish or purify, you must first choose the right type of incense. It can be a stick, a cone or in crystal form. Second, you need to decide which of the two methods of burning to use: a censer or a common incense holder or burner. Finally, allow the smoke to rise, then you can begin.

Remember how the simple process of lighting incense or a candle becomes a ritual in itself when you make yourself part of the magik.

Bell

This is a divine instrument attuned to the vibrations within energy. Traditionally used in Wicca for opening and closing rituals, it contains great feminine power which can be unleashed to ward off evil, guard the home or invoke nature spirits and positive energies.

Broom

The broom can sweep away negative energies before and after a ritual, and increase the flow of positive energy into the home. A temple should never lack a broom, and that broom should be set aside from the other household equipment, for it is a sacred ritual tool that will empower the magik performed.

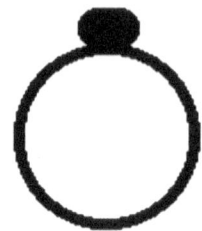

Jewellery

The wearing of silver will aid in the pursuit of psychic abilities. Knowing this, you could fashion a talisman or seal and wear it as a piece of jewellery. In Wicca one wears a necklace with a pentagram for protection and magikal inspiration. The same principle can be used in your rituals. You could wear a silver ring to enhance your energy, or a necklace with a talisman inscribed on its surface.

Inside the witch's cupboard

I have included below a shopping list of tools that will cater for almost every spell or ritual. A well-stocked witch's cupboard will give you more time to focus on the rituals, instead of having to go out each time for the things you are missing.

- a censer
- 10 candles of each colour
- 40 white candles
- 1 candle snuffer
- 6 candle holders (various sizes)
- 4 identical candle holders (for circle use only)
- 3 cords of each colour (sizes ranging from 15–30 cm)
- 2 bowls and measuring cups
- a ready supply of salt and water
- 4 glass containers with screw-on lids
- a mirror

- black ink (not water-based)
- several types of crystals
- white cotton material
- parchment paper
- incense sticks and holder
- aromatherapy oils and burner
- needle and thread
- pentacle
- wine (ritual use)

Once you have chosen the tools you wish to work with, it is time to perform the necessary jewellery-cleansing and tool-consecration rituals. This is done to rid these objects of any negativity and evil that may be attached to them, and to purify them for the use of magik.

Cleansing jewellery

Holding the jewellery between the palms of your hands, picture your energy going into the items and taking away all negativity, and say:

I cleanse you of all impurities
May you be worn in the highest of light
May you protect and guide me in all that is right
So mote it be.
OR
The Goddess rides above the night sky,
Below the God is found
Each send healing light to surround,
The jewellery that I have found.

Tool consecration

Set up your altar with the following: frankincense, salt, water and a white candle. Then cast a circle (method to follow) with the tools placed in the centre of the altar, and say:

I stand before you now, God and Goddess,
As one of the children of the light
Watch over and bless,
While I consecrate and perform this rite.
I take this candle to it I light.
By the flame that burns. Let evil be set to flight.
With the incense smoke, fill the air!
Dispel all negativity, that the tools bear.
I mix and stir the water and salt,
In forming a holy ale
To cleanse the (name of tool), to charge it full of light
Protected always, within the God and Goddess' sight.
I thank thee, Lord and lady,
For witnessing this rite
Until we meet again
Blessed be!

- Run the tools separately through each elemental representation as you speak their words, taking them through the flame (fire), then the smoke (air) and into the salted water (earth and water).

Magikal names

The ancient Egyptians believed that there was great power in a name and, like those before us in Wicca, we too believe in such power. In fact, when initiated into this faith, the individual adopts a new name, a Wiccan name to be used only while performing magikal duties. It is common in many magikal practices to adopt a new name that signifies power to whomever it is bestowed upon. The mechanics behind a magikal name are simple: they involve lining up your birth number with that of your name so they create a harmony, a balance if you will, by making both numbers equal. Numerology tells us that each number holds a different energy, and you are seeking a balance with your birth frequency, since that is your closest connection to the universal consciousness. Everything is energy, and finding your true power requires adopting a name with the same numerological significance as your date of birth, your unique blueprint. It is referred to as a magikal name because, when you are supported from within yourself, energy can flow through you freely, and that is when true magik begins.

Begin by writing your first name. Then, using the chart below, write the corresponding number under each letter.

1	2	3	4	5	6	7	8	9
A	B	C	D	E	F	G	H	I
J	K	L	M	N	O	P	Q	R
S	T	U	V	W	X	Y	Z	

Birth name: _____

Corresponding numbers: _____

Date of birth: ____/____/_____

Then fill in your date of birth. When complete, add up the numbers of your name, then separately add up the numbers of your date of birth. You will have two separate numbers, probably both double-digit numbers. Add the two digits of your name number to come up with your name number. The same applies to calculating your birth number.

To give an example, I will use the name Joanne and the date of birth 16/03/1973:

Birth name: J O A N N E
Corresponding numbers: 1 + 6 + 1 + 5 + 5 + 5 = 23; 2 + 3 = 5
Date of birth: 1 + 6 + 0 + 3 + 1 + 9 + 7 + 3 = 30; 3 + 0 = 3

It is unlikely that your name number will be the same as your birth number, as in the above example where the name number is 5 and the birth number is 3. But this can happen, as in the next example using the name Jane and the same date of birth:

Birth name: J A N E
Corresponding numbers: 1 + 1 + 5 + 5 = 12; 1 + 2 = 3

Now both numbers are 3 and so in balance. You cannot change your date of birth so, if your name number is not the same as your birth number, you need to find another name. You can either alter your birth name by adding or subtracting letters, such as by changing Joanne to Jane above, or adopt a new name for your magikal practices, finding a name whose number matches your birth number.

See Appendix A (Magikal numbers) for a list of the individual characteristics of the numbers from one to nine.

Once you have found your magikal name, it is time to consider initiating yourself into the circle of magik. This is what my tradition is called. It represents everything spiritual and magikal, allowing for self-expression and belief in what rings true for you, not what you are told. Don't be misled, for you can initiate yourself. Ask yourself this: If not, then who initiated the first? Initiation is like an affirmation of your beliefs. You only need to be open to experience: magik will do the rest.

Self-initiation

Initiation is a ritual that makes your commitment to the universal power/God and Goddess and extends your dedication to the secret arts. To prepare for the ritual, it is best to fast for a day before, or only consume organic foods such as fruits and vegetables. Gather a rope, blindfold, bell, one gold candle and some incense (preferably frankincense) or white sage, both excellent at clearing unwanted energies and raising the vibration of any space. Set up an altar within a circle to be cast later and then, approximately an hour beforehand, take a long bath to cleanse yourself. Add the oils bergamot, myrrh and rosemary. Once you have bathed, proceed to the temple skyclad. Standing in front of the altar, light the gold candle and the frankincense, while leaving the candles unlit for the God (black) and the Goddess (white) until mentioned in the ritual. Run the incense through your auric field to eliminate any negative energy that may still be attached to you. Now it is time to cast the circle, using the gold candle to light the cardinal points. Once it is cast, you can begin the initiation.

Initiation ritual

I stand here unsure of what I face,
Ringing the mighty bell three times
I call about my fiery friends,
Rid me of my fear! Rid me!

Now place the blindfold over your eyes and say:

I wait for my eyes to open,
I wait for my lord and lady
Here as I am, a golden flame
My strength is my belief,
Show me the old ways

Now tie your hands together; it is not important how they are bound together, just that they are. Symbolism is the key. While saying the following, kneel to the God and Goddess and meditate as you transcend, visualising what is to come:

I stand in darkness,
Pure of thought and belief
Take thee! In love and light.
So mote it be!

Remove the blindfold and ring the bell three times, moving your arms up and down. Pick up the athame and place it near the rope between your two hands. Then say:

I kneel now to the God and Goddess,
A believer in your divine ways
Struggling to be free, free from my past life

Through the circle of magik, I am now free!

Still holding the athame, move it through the rope, setting yourself free. Holding your hands high, say:

Reborn into the life of magik.
So shall I dedicate thy self to worship.
The God and Goddess, Lord and Lady
Walk in the footsteps of light and love.
May all spirits guide and guard me, as I their secrets
In and out of the circle of magik.
Love is now my law and bound is my faith.
From this point forward, call me (magikal name)
In my life now seen,
So mote it be.

Ring the bell three times and snuff out the gold candle. Now light the black and white candles you have for the God and Goddess and say:

I bring into this circle my soul, into the magik my faith
Out of this my life, Lord and Lady, shall there be and is
The acquisition of knowledge, of magik and past
Within the circle of magik, is where I shall be cast.

Within the circle, meditate on your life and the goals you have. Once you have finished, say:

I bless this day, thanking the God and Goddess
For their attendance, in performing this rite
The circle was cast, now close …
So mote it be!

Part II

What comes naturally

Chapter 4

Awakening the Third Eye

I can only tell you what may potentially open up your third eye. It is up to you to apply and expand your awareness to encompass the unlimited possibilities within your inner self. When delving into any unknown field, move with a little scepticism but don't let that keep you from what may seem impossible to achieve. The third eye represents the acquisition of knowledge, the thirst for answers and the pursuit of enlightenment. Opening such a doorway into your soul will symbolically signal your desire to explore your capabilities within your hidden senses, enabling you to make greater progress in your magikal work. The first technique will start the process of eliminating any false concepts and enable you to clear your mind even in the most mundane situations. Awakening your third eye will heighten your senses so that you will able to use them for psychic or magikal means. Enhancing your awareness of your surroundings is the first issue to address.

Illusion or beauty

Before we proceed, I'll give an example to explain the use of this technique. You may walk through a park and see the trees and birds, smell the air and feel the breeze. As you continue to stroll, you see a family by the river and their children at play nearby. There is nothing wrong with this scene, but what is lacking is the life and energy at play. Seeing the beauty in all living things is the key element to awakening the third eye. When your awareness grows, instead of *seeing* the trees you will feel as if they are part of you, that the whole park is an extension of your senses. When you come across another person, instead of seeing their physical appearance you will see only their inner beauty, their soul.

The process is simple. All you need to do is open up your mind and clear it of any thoughts. At first you may have to fixate on a particular medium before you can achieve any results, but in time you will be able to achieve this sense of enlightenment by will alone. Focus on a photograph of a face. Try not to strain to see the beauty within; usually you will first see this in their eyes, which are linked to the soul. Pull your thoughts aside from what you know and what you perceive and look away from any physical defects. You are looking for the person's inner beauty, encouraging it to shine through. You will notice that the facial features of this individual are becoming more defined, as if they are taking shape. After gazing for some time, changes in this person will become more apparent, meaning that you can now see their true potential, the person they are behind any facade they may show the world. The face will now seem as if it were glowing. This is the energy being emitted from that individual.

Everyone has different energy around them, and what you see for one person may not be what you see from another. It is important at this stage to focus on the beauty and perfect this. Later on I will go further into the process of seeing these energies. Use this technique with all living things. When there is a life force behind something, seeing the beauty in that lifeform is the first step to broadening your awareness and expanding the reach of your third eye.

Clearing false images of the truth and relating only to what now seems evident is not enough! Let me take you aside from the third eye for a brief moment ... Whether you are channelling, performing magik, healing or even entering into meditation, there is a fundamental state that must be achieved before any of these are practised. This is known as serenity, the place where your mind is set free from thought, a safe haven if you will. Being able to achieve this sense of peace and quiet within your mind is essential and should become second nature. If you can will an event to transpire, then your thoughts are acting as a machine behind your willpower, giving it direction. Having wild thoughts running free will prevent any results from being achieved. Especially when attempting to open the third eye, you are opening a link from your subconscious to your conscious mind, allowing yourself to receive prophetic images, and if your mind is cluttered this will cloud any messages that may come through. A method of clearing your thoughts is now to come. Understandably, this technique isn't easy, but with practice you will notice a change in the way you process incoming thoughts and how your progress will escalate once you are able to put a lock on your mind.

Locking thought

At night, light a single black candle. Its flame should be the only source of light within the room. Black is the symbol for thoughts, and the burning of this candle represents the burning of the thoughts you wish to clear from your mind. Close your eyes and, like the room, picture your mind being black, shrouded in darkness, while visualising a single light far away in the distance. This is the candle. Although you cannot see it, you know that it is there, just like your thoughts. Once this connection has been set up, sit quietly as your thoughts enter your mind. When a thought makes its presence known, see it in a material state, that is, visualise the thought as an object. Whether it is about a shopping list, a party or a close friend, see them all in a concrete form. See the shopping list, the party venue, your friend's face. The key here is to process each thought as it comes in by giving it a life of its own and then dismissing it, sending the invading thought off to the candle flame in the distance. When you have materialised a thought, concentrate solely on its relevance and give it time to be acknowledged. Then encircle it with light and send it away. Keep repeating this until you have processed each thought.

You could spend a lifetime grabbing one of a thousand thoughts that enter your mind and sending it away, but this won't happen. What you are actually doing is conditioning your mind to process the incoming thoughts, training your subconscious to automatically filter their relevance. You will find that as you materialise and dismiss each major thought coming in, the number and frequency of those thoughts begin to diminish. The more often you enter this plane, the sooner you are able to dismiss the first thought, and the more effective this technique will become. As your mind begins to quieten and the thoughts no longer exist, you will feel serenity.

The third technique also involves the use of a little magik and symbolism, but in relation to the unlocking of your subconscious mind, rather then the locking of unwanted thoughts. For this you will have the aid of a magik seal, a spell woven between time and space, as if oneness can be achieved in a moment. The timed seal of eye is what I call the key to your journey, which in time will allow all your inner knowledge to come together, enabling you to see clearly. Here I give you a tool that opens you to experiencing all that is necessary in order to achieve your truth, your true nature, in accordance with your higher self. The seal is designed to cast a web around your consciousness, through a talisman created out of words. You can either wear or bury this talisman once you have completed the ritual, to increase its influence. The choice is yours, but this technique will work just as well if you leave the seal where it lies on the next page.

Timed seal of eye

Closing your mind before you begin this ritual is essential. Luckily, after completing the last technique you will already be able to do so, making it easier to follow this process. Look into the seal, focusing on its centre for some time. As you do this, it will cast a circle of words around your life, opening up the hidden potential and desire, which is the magik you do not have! This will unlock the unseen abilities you possess. Not straining your gaze or breaking your focus is important at this point, for you do not wish to hinder the hidden spell within. Persistence will grant you what you seek. Do this for seven days and on the seventh, when night falls, light a candle and place it upon these words. Instead of focusing on the seal, visualise the third eye opening and at the same time see your psychic potential beginning to awaken and be born.

The next method, given to me by my dear friend Melissa, will aid in the opening of the third eye; its main goal is to delve deep into the subconscious mind. This is not for magikal gain, but as a way to learn and evolve. Once you are able to gain access, you will see aspects of yourself unlock in front of your very eyes, and discover parts of your true nature you were unaware of or simply too afraid to accept.

Cradled discs

Looking at the tarot, particularly at the Three of Shields card (more commonly known as Pentacles), we can find the meaning of this technique, as it incorporates the same symbolic use of circles. Through dedication and conviction we can nurture our talents, and that is what cradled discs is all about, focusing within and developing our latent psychic abilities.

For this technique to be performed successfully there must be two individuals, the practitioner and the recipient. As with hypnosis, the practitioner guides their client through a series of stimuli, but what makes this method unique is the fact that, after the initial stages, the client is the one in control within that particular session. The practitioner is present only to help the individual discover what messages their inner self is trying to relay, to provide a link and a safe exit if the recipient feels uncomfortable with their visions. Once the dual force behind this technique is mastered, you will be able to sense what the client is experiencing, so you can guide them more effectively. Remember that what you see there and what is seen by the client may not be the same. For instance, they may have trouble seeing anything at a stage in the ritual when you can sense a male presence in the room. Having trouble with certain messages is common. The key is to know when to show them what you see.

Before beginning this ritual, you are to be seated across from one another. Holding out both arms, touch each other's pulse. Thoughts travel quickly using this technique. An alternative would be to grip each other's hands; whether you use the first or second technique, be sure not to cross your arms. The balance of energies must not be broken.

The process you take the client through is as follows:
1. Picture three circles.
2. Which one did you enter?
3. Walk around, what can you see?
4. Is it hot or cold?
5. Are you alone?

Questions to ask

Main questions
1. How does that make you feel?
2. Do you wish to leave?
3. Can you see a door/a person?
4. What colours can you see?
5. Is there a distinct smell?

When a person is sighted
1. Do you recognise them?
2. Are they male or female?
3. What are they doing/wearing?
4. Walk up to them; how do you feel?
5. Say hello; what did they say?
6. Ask if they have a message/a place to take you?
7. Did the scene change once you saw them?

When a door is sighted
1. How far is it?
2. What kind of door?
3. Is it locked/opened?
4. Can you see a key?
5. Do you wish to close the door?
6. Is there anything blocking the path to the door?

7. *Do you wish to open it?*
8. *What's behind the door?*

General questions
1. *If there's paper or book, what does it say?*
2. *There is a mirror, look into it. What do you see?*
3. *If there is a room/a path, tell them to explore it.*
4. *Does your body feel heavy or light?*
5. *What would happen if you fell?*

While you are taking them through this process, keep in mind that at anytime things may become too much for the recipient to handle, so it is essential to ask, as often as you feel it is necessary:
1. *Are you ok?*
2. *Do you wish to continue?*
3. *Would you like to leave this scene?*
4. *How are you feeling?*
5. *Do you feel afraid?*

When they wish to exit a particular scene, simply talk them out by telling them to see a door and then walk right through it. Remember, whenever the ritual gets too much, always take them back to the beginning, within the circle they first walked into. This is where you ask if they wish to continue; if not, perform the closing. Remember to make your voice softer and softer as you draw to the end.

Closing the circle
1. *Listen to my voice and put all thoughts aside*
2. *3 ... Walk calmly though the door in front of you*
3. *2 ... You find yourself in the centre of a circle, at the beginning.*
4. *1 ... Darkness is all around, images have all faded. You see an intense white light consume the circle.*

5. Awake, the ritual is now complete. Sit while you ground yourself.

Clearing your mind is one thing, now I will explain how you can take this acquired knowledge a step further. I speak of meditation, the process of centring your being and achieving inner piece. In meditation you can see visions, and make discoveries about yourself without the aid of a ritual. Work with all these methods and find which one speaks true: not every method I give will be suited for you. The one that is, however, will take you places you thought were unattainable.

Basic meditation

1. It is best to be done at night (when there are no distractions).
2. Sit comfortably in a chair, with your back straight, arms by your sides and feet planted on the ground.
3. Put some soothing music on and your favourite incense.
4. Close your eyes. Alternatively, for an open-eye meditation you gaze directly into a single white candle.
5. Clear your mind. Breathing is like a mantra: ensure you keep it in the back of your consciousness.
6. Relax your body. Start from your toes, then your feet, ankles ... and so on. Moving up slowly, relax your whole body bit by bit. Every part, joint, muscle etc.
7. Once you are completely in a state of relaxation, feel yourself let go. You are in meditation; now let it guide you.
8. At this point you can picture your special place, where you feel the most comfortable. Use this as the base from where you return and enter the meditation.
9. In closing a meditation you do the opposite. Start from above your head, move down to the crown and so on until you have awakened your body.
10. Open your eyes and ground any unwanted energy by visualising it flowing out of your feet.

The next, final technique also works with meditation. The same process applies to achieve the initial state of relaxation; the only difference is the experience that happens afterwards. It should be performed on a regular basis in order to open the third eye successfully; once it is open, you will be able to work with it not only during meditation but also with other activities.

Opening third eye meditation

With your mind already in a state of meditation, visualise a shaft of white light breaking through the Earth below and entering your body. Watch as it fills you up slowly, flowing to every facet. As it rises, a sense of unconditional love grows with it and, before it peaks, it flows towards your third eye. As it nears, you feel a tingling sensation above your brow; when the light approaches, you suddenly feel a warm or burning sensation as the shaft of light burns through the third eye. The light now penetrating your entire body, it flows through your third eye and out of your line of sight and into the sky. As all this is taking place, at the moment the light breaks through, visualise your eye actually opening for a brief moment and letting the light pass through. The light now keeps the third eye firmly open! The shaft of light has travelled through you and departed via the third eye back into the universe. Bring your focus back onto your third eye: did it remain open? This ritual should be repeated until the eye remains open without any visualisation.

To those who have become well versed in the art of meditation, with knowledge of the mind and hidden energies, I give the ritual of entering a trance. It is the next step, the final step after meditation, but a trance is not for novices. Because it delves into deeper states of consciousness, only people with well-trained minds and understanding should consider attempting it. For novices, the following is best used as reference material so as to better understand the process behind meditation.

Inducing a trance

Entering a trance state can best be described by the level of brainwave activity. Brainwaves are classified into four stages: beta, alpha, theta and delta. Beta is the wide-awake state of consciousness (SOC) in which we go about our daily routines. Alpha is the state in which we daydream, an SOC that occurs before and after sleep. Theta is classed as the sleep state, when you are in a light sleep and may still be aware of your surroundings. The final SOC is delta: this level of brainwave activity is the state of deep sleep. In this state you have no knowledge that you are asleep or of your surroundings. When looking at brainwave activity in relation to altered SOC, it is easy to see how the two go together. For instance, when going into a light meditation you will be in alpha, and when going deeper into meditation you achieve the next stage, theta. Entering a trance state, you begin in alpha for a brief moment, then remain in theta for the duration of the trance. Some mediums have been known to go further, into a deeper state in which they enter the delta brainwave pattern. This I recommend against, because you must always maintain a sense of control when inducing a trance, unless you are highly experienced in the occult field.

A description of the trance state here will suffice although, with the limitations of language, I may fail to do justice to such a technique. A phase of sleep referred to as REM-sleep (Rapid Eye Movement), offers the key to unlocking a trance. Similar to the awake state, REM-sleep occurs during breaks between the cycles of deep sleep. Best described as a light-sleep state, observation on a neuronal level will note an increase in electrical activity, whereby the individual may experience an elevated pulse rate, dreams and sometimes temporary paralysis. It seems that, to induce a trance, the medium must be a master of all facets of the mind, body and spirit, and able to surrender thought in an effort to control both physical and metaphysical states of being, so as to raise the divine flame from within.

Ritual preparation

Before starting the technique for inducing a trance you first must set up your temple, as with any other ritual. Most rituals and spells should be done in darkness with only natural lighting (a candle). But for this ritual you need a well-lit room. The intent is to induce a trance, not sleep! In a poorly-lit room it may become difficult not to doze off. The focus of this ritual will depend on the amount of light that reflects off a crystal, so you can see the importance of light here. To facilitate any altered state, be sure to burn frankincense before you begin the preparations. This is to aid psychic activity and protect you while in the trance.

Below is a checklist that will enable you to prepare for the ritual:

- It is to be performed late at night, when absolute silence can be achieved.
- Dress in comfortable clothing, either purple or white.
- Leave no distractions: turn off all electrical equipment, and make sure there's no clutter.
- A large clear-quartz crystal will be your tool; ensure it's large enough to hold in your hands and that you are able to gaze into it without strain.
- If unable to obtain a crystal, you can substitute a white candle, the flame becoming the focus; ensure all windows are closed to prevent the flame from blowing out.
- Make sure, before you begin, to clear your mind of any thoughts, to keep your focus on the task.
- For the ritual you are to be seated, with your feet planted on the ground.

Ritual: entering a trance

Begin by getting comfortable in the chair, resting your arms on your lap so that your hands form a cup. Place the crystal in the centre of the cup you have made with your hand, moving it around until the light shines from one of the corners of the crystal. Now take your attention away from the crystal and focus entirely on your breathing:

Breathe in for six ... hold ... breathe out for six.

Repeat this three to six times until you are completely relaxed, and all your thoughts have left your mind. This breathing technique is to be used throughout the ritual, on a subconscious level.

As you look back at the crystal, gaze solely at the light reflecting off it. Your awareness will begin to shift and you are no longer aware of your surroundings. While gazing (without strain) into the light, you will notice that it gets brighter as your gaze becomes deeper. Your eyes will start to tire and you will feel a slight sense of dazedness fall over your body, best described as a fuzzy/tingling sensation.

Continue to gaze at the crystal, because this is the first stage of a trance: your senses shift from outward to inward, enabling you to achieve an altered SOC. Embrace this feeling, still not letting any thoughts invade your mind. Be confident you are in control and safe, that at any time you can stop and exit the trance. Continue gazing into the light and leave all concentration aside: it is just you and the crystal. The room has faded out of your awareness, and external noise is of no concern. All your focus is upon the light reflecting off the crystal; as you go deeper and deeper into the trance, put to rest any doubts or fears because you are in control, you are yourself!

At this stage you will have felt the dazed condition spread over your entire body, as if you are as light as a feather. While continuing your breathing on a subconscious level, I will give you a mantra to keep in the back of your mind. This will enable you to remain in control of your progress and go deeper into the trance. Breathe in for six, just as you have been doing, while saying "with each breath I take," then breathe out for six while saying, "I go deeper." Continue with this until all you need to say is "deeper" as demonstrated below:

With each breath I take … I go deeper and deeper into a trance
Each breath I take …   Go deeper, deeper and deeper
Each breath …   Deeper, deeper, deeper and deeper

As you do this, your focus does not shift from the light shining off the crystal. All that you are doing is adding the mantra onto your breathing pattern, in order to stimulate greater depth into an altered SOC. You will notice your energy has begun to increase far more rapidly than it would in a meditation; you are not even conscious of your body or the space you occupy. At this stage, fears and anxieties can stall your progress! It is natural to feel energy surging through you, but any thoughts other than the mantra will inhibit your trance. When you reached this point you are well into a trance and, in order to remain in this SOC, you must let go, trust in yourself and your abilities, and trust that you are well protected and safe from harm.

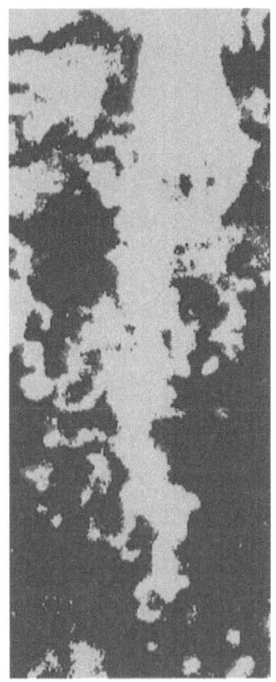

If you have been able to let go, if you have felt energy flow over your entire body, a shift in the trance occurs when you achieve a deeper level. To this point, you have continued to gaze at the light reflecting off the crystal, repeating the mantra subconsciously as you breathe. When the shift occurs, although you're gazing at the light and breathing as usual, you are unaware of those things. Your awareness expands to the size of the room, and so does your energy, until you feel no limit to the end of your awareness and your being. At this stage you envision a purple light ("violet flame" in spirituality, as previously illustrated) in front of you; watch as it comes closer towards you. The purple light penetrates your skin and emerges from your third eye: you are now in a deep trance and ready to receive.

When inducing a trance, never strain or push yourself to achieve something you're not ready for. Practise the ritual for entering a trance over a period of seven weeks, keeping a record of every session. In no time you will be making progress. Although this ritual for trance induction is for those who are experienced in altered SOC, each time you practise this technique, be sure to insert a particular word, a subconscious suggestion, when you have achieved a deeper level of trance. The next time you induce a trance, all you will have to do is repeat the breathing exercise and say that word (make it something uncommon) and you will be back in the same state.

Chapter 5

Natural power

Before you consider practising low magik, an extensive background in the power that can be harnessed within nature is essential. Developing an understanding of the energies that are found in simple objects such as cords, brooms and stones will enable you to form respect for that power and the gift of magik. Anyone with a little training can perform a spell, although they will not truly connect and exert influence over their environment. Learning the extent of your own power, and overcoming the hidden obstacles of failure and disbelief that have been conditioned upon society, can open up a flood of untapped energy within yourself that, when directed by your own desire, becomes far more powerful than the use of any spell. Like you, every living thing has its own energy vibration, whether it is a tree or a wand carved from wood. I will demonstrate in this section how to utilise the potential of these energies, through your own will and direct influence over the living energy that is within all things.

The first technique is a simple exercise that will enable you to develop strong intuition and open the door to the magikal you. Begin by collecting thirteen different types of crystals of relatively the same size, thirteen envelopes and a pen and notepad. Before using the crystals, it is best to cleanse them of any impurities that may cause you to receive the wrong type of energy vibration. With the use of a little salt and water, the following crystal-cleansing ritual will do the trick.

Crystal cleansing

I take this salt, this water
In making a holy ale
To the salt, drive out impurities
To the water, wash away negativity
For the crystals, to lay
Cleanse and purify
Ready to release you energies
On this very day!
By the Earth, Moon and sea
I call the Goddess to be with me.
May You send Your healing light
To cleanse and purify these crystals
With all Your divine might.
I leave them with You to care
For when You leave
They shall be clear of all negativity.

Once the crystals have been properly prepared, place each one into a separate envelope and number each one on the outside, then seal them shut. On the notepad draw up a small table or use the one that follows.

Crystal reading exercise

Envelopes	Attempt A	Attempt B	Attempt C	Attempt D	Contents of envelope	Correct attempts
1						
2						
3						
4						
5						
6						
7						
8						
9						
10						
11						
12						
13						

Sit down in silence and relax your body by deep breathing or meditation. Once all thoughts have escaped your mind, close your eyes and pick up each envelope, one at a time and not in sequence, and place it between your hands. Let it sit there for a while and wait for any emotions or sensations you may get from that particular crystal, then open your eyes and jot down the impressions you received under the correct envelope number in the table. Repeat this process until you have made three or four attempts to identify each crystal. When the exercise is complete, open each envelope and write down the type of crystal and its qualities in the column headed "Contents of envelope." You may have received a message or impression about the particular qualities of the crystals. Here is an example of a partly-completed table:

Envelopes	Attempt A	Attempt B	Attempt C	Attempt D	Contents of envelope	Correct attempts
1	gold & riches	halt/ hinder	strength	power	tiger eye: power & manliness	3
2	coldness & despair	blue & water	tranquillity	healing	agate: health & change	2
3	fear & sadness	the heart	blood stone	n/a	blood stone: emotions & health	3 (identified)
4	passion	truth & positivity	healing	conflict & darkness	amethyst: healing & intuition	1
5	hatred	red streams	blood stone	love & passion	malachite: uncertainty & sleep	0
6	orange & warmth	tension	citrine	happiness	citrine: cleansing & hope	3 (identified)
cont.						

This illustrates the type of impressions you will receive from the envelopes and how they translate to the type of crystal concealed inside. Note that with envelope number three not all the attempts were used: when you are getting a strong impression, go with it, trust your intuition!

The next technique requires only a little effort on your part and is something you can use time and time again. When you work with energy and the power you can raise from it, you become aware of the side effects including the problems that can occur if you do not earth/discard the unused energy. For instance, when you perform a healing, after the client has departed a part of them may still be built up within you, and if you do not release that dead energy then you may become ill. The ritual below will take you on a little journey to release unwanted energies and replenish the void with the natural energy found in nature.

Energy release – grounding yourself

Go for a walk until you see a tree which appears full of life, its branches reaching high above the ground, the leaves glittering in the sun and the trunk rising beyond the sky. Walk up to this tall, strong tree and sit with your back against its trunk to rest. Imagine the tree is all that exists, so nothing else comes into your mind or into your line of sight. Release all your tension, doubts and negativity into the tree. A moment later you will notice that everything that was bothering you has disappeared and the tree has begun to replace the negative void with love. Without shifting your sense of calm, you realise that you have achieved a sense of peace and uplifting energy with ease. It has become hard not to smile. Now stand and thank the tree for its gift of serenity.

This technique can be used in reverse, for example, to keep a plant from dying. All that is required on your part is to sit close to it and project unconditional love into the plant.

There are many myths that surround the occult and it can be hard not to get swept up in all the nonsense. It is not the case that you have to perform a grand ritual for months on end to achieve your goal, or even perform a ritual at all; as you've seen, the power that lies within is far greater than the use of a ritual whose meaning may not be apparent. A common myth is that of the weather: sunny day = happiness, rainy day = sadness. The truth is simple: on one hand, a sunny day does bring light to darkness, answers to questions and so on, but in regards to a rainy day, the myths are far from the truth. Rain symbolises the washing away of pain, wealth, cleansing and change, and when it rains on a special occasion this actually brings good fortune. To improve your relationship with the elements, the chant below will cause the sun to come out from behind dark clouds and can stop rain and create a bright and sunny day.

Sunny day
I invoke thee! I invoke thee! I invoke thee!
By the four winds of creation, earth, air, fire, water
By the eternal spirit, God and Goddess divine.
Bring forth light, into day
From clouds of dark, to sky of blue
Be gone clouds, from my eyes two.
Sun shine from above, to thee down below
From dark to light, now shall it be so
As I will it, so mote it be!

*I invoke thee (the sun) – this part of the chant is to enable you to form a rhythmic breathing pattern that is essential to performing the ritual.

To expand on elements, I have included below a chart that outlines their individual characteristics and what they represent. One of the most diverse and easily-learnt practices of witchcraft is now at your fingertips, and with no trouble you will able to find the main ingredients for your spells with nature, fundamentally, the elements. See also Elemental magik later in this chapter.

Elements

	earth	air	fire	water
cardinal	north	east	south	west
energy	nurturing	intuitive	protective	healing
colour	green	yellow	red	blue
symbol	shield	sword	wand	cup
tool	crystal	censer	candle	cauldron
ritual use	fertility, stability, prosperity, growth, strength	travel, message, knowledge, study, recovery	purity, strength, banishment, courage, sex	cleansing, sleep, inner sight, love, friendship
elemental	Gnomes	Sylphs	Salamanders	Undines
archangel	Auriel	Raphael	Michael	Gabriel

Your main goal should now be to rise above the myths about magik and master your own will, increasing the force behind the rituals you will perform later. Discover which area you excel in, the spiritual or the physical side of magik, and this will give you an idea of what methods to use in order to improve the power of your will. Even if you are a novice, unclear of your capabilities, experiment with several forms of magik until you find your calling. I have included below two short but effective techniques that with a little persistence can lead to making greater strides in your magikal training.

Traffic lights
The first technique is an act of deliberately influencing your environment, removing the mental blocks in your mind to unlock the possibilities which are obtainable by the pure extension of your desires. The main objective is to manipulate the colour of the traffic light from red to green before you arrive at an intersection. As you approach the lights, all that should be in your mind is a picture of those lights and, as you perform the exercise below, visualise yourself continuing to drive through the intersection.

Inhale the red for six seconds, hold ...

Then exhale the green for six

Like my breathing exercise, what makes this unique is the key to changing the lights. The key principle is to see a red car pass through the lights at the exact moment they are desired to change from red to green. This symbolises the end of the red light and the beginning of the green. When practising this technique regularly, you may find that a red car passes through each time without the need to visualise it.

The second technique coincides with the art of divination known as scrying; this will be the first of many rituals given for you to test your psychic capabilities and further train your expanding willpower. The art of scrying has always been one of my favourite pastimes, for you can practise it several times and each time experience a deeper meaning for seeing into other dimensions. The method I give can be adapted to other techniques of scrying such as crystal balls, fire and mirror gazing.

Scrying

The dead of night is the best time for this ritual to take place, for you need absolute silence and complete darkness. This ritual is great for solitary practitioners, but can also be done by a small group of no more than three people (if in a group, it is vital that you hold hands to connect your energies). Begin by clearing the temple of all clutter and furnishings so that there is only a table and enough chairs to perform the ritual. Then gather black ink (not water-based), a large bowl and 1 to 2 litres of water. Place the bowl in the centre of the table, adding enough water so that the bowl is three-quarters full (leaving room to prevent the water from spilling). Then add the black ink to the water, ensuring that the two merge together, creating a reflective surface. The remainder of the water is placed beside the table to wash your hands after the ritual, getting rid of any energy that may attach to you.

Once the ritual is set up, sit in darkness with just enough light to see the surface of the water. You may wish to increase your energy first through meditation; if not, go ahead and visualise a golden light surrounding yourself or the group, saying:

Around me now
Stands a wall of light
Protect me whilst
Performing this rite.
Mirror, mirror, scry for me
Mirror, mirror, let me see
Mirror of moonlight skies
Allow me to see
The visions that pass by my eyes.

Now, repeat only the second verse while gazing into the bowl, and do not remove your glance or obstruct your focus. Remember to keep your mind free from thought at all times, so as to allow a vision to reveal itself.

After some time the water will seem to shift, until it appears to spin rapidly as if it were going to overflow. It is important to remain calm and maintain your gaze (to look away now will stop the transition), for you may see brief images of people and towns as you become ready to see whatever will appear. Abruptly the images will fade and the water will slow to a halt; at this point you are to state your purpose or what you wish to see, at the same time repeating the second verse. Continue gazing into the bowl, this time directing your desire into it. The water will again shift, but instead of passing images you will see fog rise from the centre of the bowl, moving outwards until it flows over the edge onto the table. Although you must keep gazing at the water, maintain a sense of control, for if you become too receptive you may endure a blackout. Don't strain to see, just keep at it and you'll succeed. When the fog clears, an image will start to form, and you will see the vision that you requested. Remember, you see what you want to see, and you should have been specific about times and dates etc. The image doesn't always come through as clearly as we would like; just repeat "Mirror, mirror, scry for me, Mirror, mirror, let me see" and in no time the images will become more defined. Keep practising this ritual like any other, and the end result will be worth the time you invest in it.

The next technique combines all that has been learnt so far, the use of your will and the direction of energy, and also the manipulation of your environment through your desire to bring about change.

Cord magik

Cord magik, sometimes called knot magik, is the use of knots to store built-up energy and power that can later be released with great force to bring change and alter your environment. Cords are used in many ways, and their usage is widespread in witches' covens. They can be hung in the home to promote harmony and luck, or situated in an office to bring profit and success. On a more personal note, you might tie something of importance (such as your book of shadows) with a cord, so that when loaned to another its return is guaranteed. When deciding what colour the cord should be, check Appendix B (Colours) at the back of this book. Due to its magikal significance, colour plays an important role in cord magik. For instance, if you have a number of cords, it is easier to identify which cord is for what purpose when using the right colour. As for the length of the cord, this depends completely on the purpose, for example, whether it is to be worn around the neck or tied around a book. I suggest an all-purpose length of 35 centimetres, with knots 2 to 5 cm apart. When tying the knots, start from one end and work your way down, moving from side to side and excluding the third knot, which is tied in the centre of the cord to create a balance.

This is shown in the diagram below:

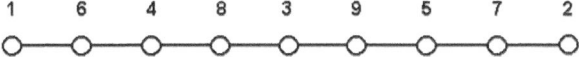

Cord magik should be done when your energy is at its highest peak. It is best to cast a circle and meditate on the purpose of creating the cord; while doing this, concentrate on building up your energy so that you can store a greater amount of power within the knots. You will find several techniques for building up your energy in chapters 6 and 7. Before tying each knot, direct all your energy to it, at the same time keeping the purpose of the cord in mind – then seal it! Make the knot tight. Tie all the knots with conviction, saying:

By knot of one, the magik's begun!
By knot of two, it shall be true!
By knot of three, power has cometh from me!
By knot of four, to this I store!
By knot of five, this spell's alive!
By knot of six, I have fixed!
By knot of seven, treasures I'll be given!
By knot of eight, it will be fate!
By knot of nine, what's done is mine!

When you wish to realise the power from the cord, it is best to untie the knots one day at a time, making sure you untie them in the same order you tied them. Follow the same process of casting a circle and putting in the same amount of concentration/energy.

Finally, before you read any further or rush to the back where all the spells are, consider the use of sympathetic magik: in this case, the use of the witch's broom to cause change. It may appear foolish to rely on a broom to work your magik but, as with any ritual tool, the broom is all you need for a ritual to succeed. Below I give an extensive list of easy methods of using the magik broom, especially designed for people with hectic lifestyles, those who do not have the time to set up a ritual or cast a spell. This will enable you to obtain your desires with only a few simple techniques of practical magik.

Broom magik

The broom represents all that is domestic, cleanliness and magikal protection. Knowing this will help you understand the power and magikal capabilities behind the use of this old friend.

Unfolding Magik

It is important to keep a special broom for the use of magik, separate from the everyday broom used for household cleaning, just as you would not chop carrots with your athame. The broom should be made of natural materials with no plastic handle or fixtures, and its style should reflect balance, although the design and decoration of your ritual broom are entirely up to you. The broom has many uses that can easily take the place of a complex ritual or spell. Here is a list of some old and new methods of working with brooms and the energies that can be raised by the use of broom magik.

Enchanted broom

- A broom near the main entrance will protect the home.
- Pointing a broom towards the main entrance will direct evil away from the home.
- Keeping a broom against the back door while away will work against theft.
- To guard the house while you are away for a ling time, cross two new brooms at the main entrance.
- Lay a broom in the threshold of a door to increase spiritual activity; pointing the handle slightly into your temple will aid in communicating with spirits.
- Old brooms bring bad luck to a new home, for they take away the harmony from the previous house, causing the energies within to be disturbed.

- Placing a broom beneath the bed will protect you while you sleep and aid in the experience of prophetic dreams.
- Cross two brooms to dispel negative energy.
- Remove negative energy from the temple by swinging a broom around over your head at staff length.
- To rid the house of unwanted entities, sweep the corners of the ceiling and especially inside the archway of each door.
- While outside, sway a broom high above your head to bring rain; holding it steady and visualising it as a metal rod will call up a thunderstorm.
- Keeping a broom in your bed will cause it to remain empty.
- Riding a broom will promote fertility.
- To remove unwanted guests, place a broom bristle-side up against a door. If they refuse to leave, drive a fork into its bristles and soon they will depart. (The fork having the same shape as the broom symbolises the strength of your desire.)
- Carry a small novelty broom with you for luck.
- Tying a red ribbon around two brooms will bring a new love into your life.
- Place money in the bristles of a broom for prosperity.
- To drop a broom promotes change and the acceptance of change.
- A thin broom is used for the creation of magik.
- Brushing the bristles of a broom will aid in beauty.
- Hearing the sweeping of a broom represents insight and intuition.
- To symbolise growth, lay a broom on the ground and jump over it; this can also be used to increase a harvest.
- Keeping a broom in an office will clear thoughts and create a harmonious environment.

- Washing a broom will remove dead energy from the household and bring positive change.
- Planting a broom in the soil bristle-side up represents growth and aids in the health and wellbeing of your plants.
- Grip the handle of a broom to help relieve stress and anxiety.
- Sweeping will remove all negative energy within a circle.
- A broom can be used in place of a wand to summon energy.
- Breaking a broom symbolises tragedy and loss.

As you can see, the broom is a valuable asset in the practice of magik; with only a little visualisation you will achieve results. Now that you have experienced the practical side of sympathetic magik, you can perform low magik with greater understanding and control. Remember that magik is only as strong as your desire to obtain your objective.

For the continual development of your magikal skills, I have included the use of another medium, the tarot. By utilising the same principles, you will be able to identify and apply what you have already learnt.

Tarot magik

Tarot magik is in many respects different from tarot reading. The tarot cards are used to find answers past, present or in the near future. With magik you use those cards as you would a talisman, runes, a pentacle or atheme. They are a symbolic representation so, when referring to the tarot cards, you are symbolising the desired outcome through a particular spread of cards. For a reading, shuffle the cards, pick three using your intuition and lay them out. Depending on the question or need at the time, the cards either represent the past, present and future, or the past, obstacles and the future.

For magik you do the same: shuffle your cards while stating your purpose then, instead of laying them out, put the deck down. Now intuitively choose three cards that respond to the needs of the spell and relate to the desired outcome. Once all three cards are spread out in a triangle in front of you, meditate on your goal for a moment. When awakened from that state, move your hand over the cards, visualising the manifestation of your need, then go back into meditation. In this ritual you do not focus on the outcome, but place your awareness on the cards themselves. See them work together as one, an unstoppable force that will carry out the request you have put before it. Start by focusing on each card at a time, reaffirming its meaning and its relevance to this spell, moving along until you have seen all three cards in their true forms. To bring it to a close, focus all three as one and direct this to your desire, not willing it but seeing it take form and becoming truth.

To help you find the most suitable card, I have listed the tarot cards and their meanings. Work with them all and not just a few; they are all connected and in some cases their interpretations flow into each other. You will see after working with the tarot that, no matter how many times you deal with a certain card, it will always bring something. That's where you should begin your reading. Be shown and go from there!

Minor arcana cards

	Shield	Sword	Wand	Cup
King	stability	bravery	passion	imagination
	reliable	knowledge	voice	falsehood
	illusion	dispute	determination	artistic
Queen	insight	uncertainty	clarity	honesty
	expression	imagination	jealousy	change
	generosity	strong willed	compassion	illusion

Unfolding Magik

	Shield	Sword	Wand	Cup
Knight	maturity	dispute	adventure	news
	alone	change	absence	movement
	illusion	doubt	separation	deception
Page	study	wisdom	potential	chance
	challenge	thought	loyalty	reflection
	wellbeing	discretion	faith	trust
Ten	risk	hope	force	happiness
	belief	anguish	stress	reward
	opportunity	blind sighted	loss	peace
Nine	foresight	prevention	discover	cheer
	gain	delay	recovery	abundance
	danger	suffering	obstacle	overwhelm
Eight	crafting	bound	action	bounty
	vanity	conflict	progress	past
	skill	pain	failure	withdrawn
Seven	anxiety	reason	competition	delusion
	hidden	hope	victory	fear
	growth	decision	emotional	desire
Six	envy	solitude	fear	memory
	enrichment	journey	success	future
	blind sight	barrier	strives	ideas
Five	loss	struggle	goals	regret
	trouble	fool	grounding	innocence
	restriction	defeat	opportunity	loss
Four	delay	recovery	harmony	alone
	disillusion	unsettling	progress	bitterness
	greed	rest	insecurity	unfulfilled
Three	dignity	discontent	initiative	solution
	talent	passion	influential	kindness
	conviction	sorrow	foundation	healing
Two	absent	trouble	courage	peace
	balance	opposition	sensitivity	harness
	pressure	centred	attainment	harmony
Ace	deceit	force	creation	wholeness
	prosperity	intellect	fortune	perfection
	restrained	destruction	talent	curiosity

I give you this as a guideline for the minor arcana cards, not the major arcana cards. This is a basis to work from, some key words to help you with reading the cards, not to instruct you in what to read and how to go about doing so. Once you have found your anchor, your level of understanding of the meaning of the major cards will come. The majority of the tarot speaks for itself; it is up to you to find its message in the current reading.

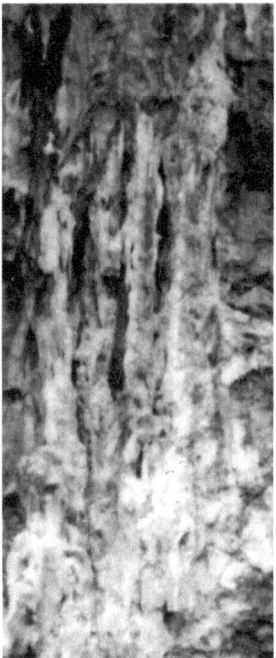

Elemental magik

In the previous section, the elements were briefly explained but their use in magik was not fully explored. I have shown the magik that lies within each element; now I will demonstrate the power of the elements and how easy and effective their magik can be. Within no time you will be able to adapt them to spells or rituals you may be performing.

Candle scrying

Stand three tall candles in a circle, a triad of power sitting in harmony with one another in similar holders, white as snow and pure of negativity; then you light the wicks. If one candle burns brighter or taller, your answer is a definite yes. When sparks shoot out of a candle, this is a definite no. Before you set up the ritual, close all windows and doors, and seal up anywhere wind may enter. This is so that this technique cannot be influenced by other means than a direct link with the divine source. The candles move according to their own desire to tell the story. The objective is to identify in which direction the candle flames rotate; usually you find "yes" is clockwise and "no" is anti-clockwise, but test both directions first with a simple yes/no question. Ask something like, "Is a circle round?" for yes and "Is my name candle?" for no; fairly obvious answers are necessary to establish the bearings for this ritual.

When this has been done, remember that the answers are more definite if the three candles all agree on the message relayed back to you. If you find that the flames remain still or move unclearly, then either take this as a maybe or ask the question again more specifically. When receiving answers from candles, you are also open to receiving messages from spirits as with any other form of scrying. The candles are just a medium, a tool through which you use your own abilities; do not let them prohibit you from delving further into the answers given.

Candle – yes and no

Using the same principles as the previous ritual, take two candles, one black and one white, and place them on the altar, ensuring that you keep them apart. Light the wicks then proceed to ask your questions, moving the candles closer together after each answer has been given. When the two candles touch, that signifies the end of the ritual, which allows the practitioner only a limited number of questions. Nothing can be certain, especially when you are referring to future predictions, and continuing a particular query may cause you to unintentionally falsify the end result.

Crystal water

Collect a smooth, clear-quartz crystal so that no shards will break off and cleanse it carefully. Then add it to a bottle of drinking water, leaving it for at least five hours. The water will now be charged and when consumed will give you energy. The same process can be used to charge water for other purposes such as magik.

Death

In ancient Egyptian culture death and the dead were referred to as the west and westerners. This uses that principle to send your love and prayer to the dearly missed, someone who lives eternally in the west. Light a candle, placing it upon a window ledge on the eastern side of the house. Then say a little prayer and your good-byes, and blow out the candle. The smoke will carry your message into the west where the soul rests.

Earthquake

This technique is used to prevent damage by an earthquake, and can also be applied to the prevention of disastrous situations that could occur in your life. It is a year-round protective spell that will keep working as long as it sits undisturbed. You can either find a small pot and fill it with fresh soil, bury a bell in the centre and keep the pot in your room or, to get the best results, plant a bell deep in the backyard to protect the household. The mechanics behind this spell are simple: balancing the onset vibrations of an earthquake with the harmonious energy emitted from the bell will encourage a positive outcome.

Hair growth

Here are two methods to aid your hair in growing. First, cut your hair about two centimetres on the night of a new moon (waxing period). The same process can be used to slow the growth of your hair, by cutting it on the night of a full moon (waning period). The second method involves buying a small plant and planting a couple of centimetres of your hair beneath it, although not directly beneath. When the plant begins to grow, so shall your hair. You can perform this on the night of a new moon to increase the chances of hair growing.

House keys

To protect the house, take a spare set of house keys and bury them under or as close to the main gate as possible. This will lock out evil and prevent negativity from entering. When you are searching for a new home, carry a set of uncut house keys and a clear quartz crystal with you. If the house is right, the keys will tell you through the power of the crystal.

Love's blind

Take two white cords of the same length and inscribe your name on one and the characteristics of a potential lover on the other. Bind them together with a red cord that is also the same length. These are to be worn either as a bracelet or coiled to form an amulet which you carry with you. The same method can be adapted to bring a friendship closer; all that it requires is to change the colour of the third cord to that of friendship (pink) and the inscriptions on the first two cords. To break the spell, simply cut the cords.

Natural empowerment

There are various methods of empowering yourself but what you need is all around you. Simply take a handful of soil and run your hands under water, or perhaps you may prefer to hold your palms over a candle flame, or stand in a strong breeze and charge yourself with natural energy. When you partake in any of these basic rituals, all that is required of you is to visualise the energy entering your body, filling your soul and merging with your entire being. This will lift your spirits and increase your hidden potential, empowering you the natural way.

Problems

To relieve stress and tension, take a single leaf in the palm of your hand and crush it. A broken leaf, when still alive, helps resolve these unwanted emotions. To balance the exchange of energy, be sure to ask for permission first before you take the leaf. A similar technique is to use soil instead. It does not matter what stimulus you use to release a problem. When discarding the leaf or soil, do it over your shoulder and don't look back. Would you wish to dwell on such unpleasantness?

Raise winds

For this technique I recommend you use sand, although fine grains of soil can work just as well. Take a handful of earth, making sure not to let any slip through your fingers. When the wind starts to pick up, blow the earth in the palm of your hand in the direction of the wind. To stop wind, face the wind and stand firm, with knife in hand. Swiftly and with no hesitation, cut into the air. Another method that works in the same way involves the use of a feather. Still facing the wind, instead of cutting through the air you slice the feather in two. The colour of the feather should correspond with the east or with the principle of halting the wind.

Sand divination

As with other forms of divination such as scrying, sand divination focuses on looking for symbols, a pattern in the grains of sand rather than faint images and visions sent by an outside force. For best results, gather a small bowl of sand by the seashore. Start by asking a question and, as you do this, make a single line in the sand, its shape being irrelevant. The line should travel through the section which holds your awareness. Once the line has been drawn, take your focus off the sand and onto the line. The answers you seek lie within that line and in the tiny grains of sand.

Storm prevention

When a fierce storm approaches, acquire a large sharp object (which will act as a vacuum) and face the storm as it travels your way. As with stopping the wind, you also cut through the air in this ritual, but you have to let the magik take you. Run towards the storm and, as you leap into the air, swing the sharp object around anti-clockwise, then stab the implement into the ground, earthing the energy.

Symbolic earth

When you cast your spells in this day and age, carving them in stone does not seem appropriate, but if you wish to have a permanent record of a particular spell then this technique is for you. Inscribe the spell or the corresponding symbols/runes in the earth, which could be soil, snow or sand. This heightens the magik and enchants the spell. Another simple method is to draw a set of symbols/runes in the sand on the seashore, and when the tide comes in it will wash away the spell, sending the magik forth.

Threshold protection

Place a line of small grains of soil unnoticeably across the threshold to ward off negativity entering the home. This also applies to the unwanted energy that may have attached itself to people who go to and from your home.

Water's edge

To ward off evil, take a bowl of water and place a knife on top of it with the blade facing outwards. If inside a room, face it towards a window. This works especially well when dealing with negative thoughts or magik that have been directed towards you. On a general note, whenever you are travelling and feel the uncertainty of evil at play, cross over water and evil will not follow. The same goes for immersing yourself in water, which cleanses you of the ties towards evil at work.

Chapter 6

Life Force

The force that flows,
Through the embodiment of existence.

There are many forms of the life force described in this book, but the actual components behind the process we call life and the universe have yet to be explored. What drives a spell? What types of energies do we invoke? How are the God and Goddess related to this? Can we actually learn to see and touch such power? And are such forces good or evil? These are the questions that will be answered in this chapter. When you combine this knowledge with your current practices, you will be able to see the entire process, from when you begin to cast a spell until after you have obtained your desired outcome.

I speak first of emotions, not quite a source of life; however, when you look closely at them, you can see the relationship they have with each other. A brief example is how you feel when you get caught up in something you love, compared to how you feel when you are sick.

Your mood, emotional state and general wellbeing are important and play a major role in your magikal work. When dealing with any form of energy, keeping a balance between the spiritual and the physical worlds is the first step. I will not tell you what foods you must eat and how to live your life, but will just give guidelines on what should be done in order to remain at a higher vibration.

Inside spells

What drives a spell? You could say we manifest a spell through the design of a desire, a wish to make it so. This is just the beginning, for our free will is the mechanics behind the magik; as we will a spell to form in this realm, our emotional state will dictate the potency of the outcome.

You cannot find love if you do not have love for yourself. You cannot heal another if you are ill, or protect your home when you do not possess inner strength. The need must be there, a connection that binds your will and your desire to achieve manifestation. This is why I strongly recommend only performing spells for yourself: casting for another will diminish the chances of the outcome being achieved.

The key that gives a spell life is simply thought. I say to my students, "First thought, then creation." The rest comes along the way. We can will an event to transpire and use our emotions to direct and drive those desires behind the spell, but to actually achieve what we set out to obtain, we must see and feel it happen.

There is no use in casting for love and in the back of your mind saying to yourself, *I'll never find someone special*. Spells are not merely words on paper nor affirmations of power; they are alive and take on a life of their own. But they cannot think for themselves: they do exactly what you will, what you want and what your thoughts direct them to do. Without a clear mind, any spell you cast will seek out precisely what you have cast, probably not in the way you would have preferred. Think of this: you cast a spell for love. For the spell to find love, you lose your job and you meet someone in the unemployment line, instead of on the street in front of the employment agency a month later.

Energy types

What types of energies do we invoke? When dealing with different types of energy, we often come to excel in one more than another, and this becomes the focus of our practices. I have composed a list of principal forms of energies so that you can identify what works best for you and when to use which types of energy.

- emotions
- colour
- spiritual
- universal
- elemental
- bodies of energy
- physical

Emotions

Out of all the forms of energy, this is the one used the most. Since emotions are not an unfamiliar source to tap into, we tend to feel more comfortable using them than we would another form of energy.

When you are channelling emotions, the key is to remember it is actually the channelling of pure emotions. These are not the real emotions that run through you. As with all energy, you must channel them through you, rather than from within you; it is unwise to use your own energy, for this would leave you weakened. Channelling an emotion is completely different in nature from feeling that particular emotion.

Colour

This is a technique I do not perform on a regular basis (refer to Appendix B for colour references). The main focus behind channelling colour is that you are able to direct its energies more easily and, when you use another technique, the energy raised will go where it is needed, rather than where you have placed it.

Spiritual

This practice is becoming more commonly used. There are several ways you may go about channelling spiritual energy and healing, and I will take you through the ways that I know to be true to me.

The first requires you to call your guides/angels to you and instruct them to show you where to place your hands on the client, through the use of your inner senses. This can lead to trust being built between you and a certain spirit which, in time, you could allow to take over the healing as if it was their own.

The next involves you channelling angelic energy through yourself as you run your hands through the client's aura; as you do this, your own energy will also be raised, increasing the effect of the energy work.

The third method is to call all the spirits/angels of the light to surround you and send you their energy. Visualise a circle of light, which is actually a circle of angels that have become a representation of the pure source of light, spinning around and directing their unconditional love into the core, which is you.

It is important to remember that, when you are invoking, channelling or raising spiritual energy, only call from the highest source of light and love. These methods are taken from those I use while performing a healing, but you can also adapt them to incorporate into your own magik.

Universal

Not like spiritual energy, universal energy refers to the channelling of the highest form of energy itself, the ultimate power, what some would call God energy. You call this energy the same way you call spiritual energy, although in this case you are bringing down pure energy, not the same type as you would channel from an entity.

Elemental

The raising of the elements and the spirits (elementals) that reside in the natural realm is very wellknown in the occult field. Especially in paganism, you will find references to those entities and various rituals for invoking them for the connection to nature they bring with the energy raised.

Earlier in the book I looked at the nature of the elements and, as you saw, they are a very powerful force to channel. Before you begin this energy work, you should find out which elemental best suits you, that is, what type of energy you relate to: an earth, air, water or even a fire spirit. Read again the information on the elements and find the one that corresponds to your true nature.

Then it is up to you how long you work with that particular elemental before moving on to the next. Keep in mind that they are as old as time and so the knowledge and energy they bring can be a little overwhelming. As in all your practices, maintaining a sense of control is the first step before continuing with what you are trying to achieve.

On a different note, you can also invoke the power or energy of a crystal. Simply hold it in the palm of your hand and channel its energy through you. Refer to Appendix C (Crystals) when choosing the appropriate crystal.

Bodies of energy

To some, this is an unfamiliar way to invoke energy, but I find it quite effective. It involves the channelling of psychic or auric energies; the only difficulty is keeping your own energy separate from the one you are channelling. This is something you should already be able to achieve if you have been practising the previous methods.

You visualise energy being channelled through your third eye into your body. Remember that the psychic energy being invoked is not your own; it is untamed psychic power you are seeking to obtain.

With the invocation of auric energy, you could end up leaving yourself drained, for you are actually channelling from your own auric field. The key is to raise your own energy vibration and, once you have done this, channel only the auric energy you have raised. This will leave you feeling more energised and also give you a powerful source of energy which you are able to direct like any other type of energy.

Physical

There are several spells in this book that involve the use of blood magik. Blood is what keeps us alive; it is called "life energy" and using its power in a ritual will increase the effect on your desired outcome.

I will never say that you must bleed in order to cast a certain spell; that is too extreme. All spells are designed so that you can incorporate whatever ingredients you prefer to use, and alter them to fit your needs or purpose. All I am doing here giving you is true magik in all its forms, so as not to hide any facet of its nature.

As with anything, with blood you must use your own judgement. You can use your own hair or tears as a replacement for blood, for they are still a part of you. We use something from our physical self to bind us to the spell and its purpose. You could easily achieve the same results by using another of the techniques I have given you to invoke energy.

Whether you decide to use blood, a lock of hair or tears to aid in the creation of a spell, keep in mind that these are just representations of raising energy. The method you use does not matter, as long as the discipline is there.

How are the God and Goddess related to this?

The true natures of the God and Goddess are ambiguous: they are neither man nor woman. They are a dual deity that embodies all the qualities of the Earth and Moon, the elements, the sky and sea, even the universe, the good as well as the evil.

It is in Wicca that we find an expansion of what can only be referred to as omnipresence, the universal consciousness. We can see how the divinity has been split in half so we can understand its true concept; it is difficult to worship an ambiguous deity and relate to it. Putting it into the two separate houses of man and woman, light and dark, the Lord and Lady, makes working with such a being more promising. Together they represent the supreme force, a higher power that is beyond our understanding.

This is how they relate to what I call the "life force." The God and Goddess are representations of universal energies and unconditional love and, in effect, they are this life force. Together they are the highest expression of light and love.

The aura

Can we actually learn to see and touch such power? Energy is at play all around us, whether we choose to acknowledge it or not. It surrounds every living organism. Where there is life, there are energy fields that emanate from its existence. These are auras.

Learn to see energy

Energy sighting is like looking through a dirty window. At first all you see is whatever is outside, the physical reality. Then, when you unfocus your eyes, all you can see is the dirt on the window, the unseen/hidden realm, instead of what is outside.

Start by holding up your hand and gazing at the gaps between your fingers, making sure you unfocus your eyes. Do not strain to see the energy; just relax your gaze and practise until you make progress. It is unrealistic to expect a vast array of colour to become evident. You will most likely see a fuzzy blur between each finger, which may become a clear field of energy.

When you are in the company of a like-minded friend, get them to stand up straight against a white wall. Make sure the light in the room does not cast any shadows on their body, as this could lead to a false sighting of an energy field. Again relax your gaze as you focus on the outer edges of the subject. The first place you are likely to sight an energy field is around the head, for it is the closest point on the body to the third eye.

Some of the techniques in the section 'Awakening the third eye' in chapter four can aid in seeing such energy. One in particular is the channelling of that very energy to aid in seeing what is hidden from your gaze. Since you should be well-versed in energy work by now, doing this exercise will come naturally.

Before you begin to gaze on a particular subject, relax, slow your breathing to a rhythm and then call on the purest (universal) energy to flow through their body. This technique will cleanse as well as lift the individual's vibration, allowing you to see the energy more effectively.

Learn to touch energy

But how is it possible to touch something that isn't there? If we can breathe in air and be aware of its presence, why is it so hard to conceive of the concept of hidden energies? On the other hand, believing in them and being able to touch them are different things. Can you let go of what you know to be fact, in order to grasp the notion that you are about to touch a part of your reality that was always there, but remained hidden from your normal train of thought?

Hold both hands out in front of you in a vertical position, about two centimetres apart, your palms parallel. You can also use this part of the technique to view the energy field between both hands.

Slowly move your hands away from each other to about 30 cm apart, and then move them slowly back together. As you do this a breeze will flow between your hands and, as you draw them closer together, your palms will become warmer. This is because your palms are the energy centres of the body and when working with such energies they tend to heat up.

With your hands in the same position, again move them slowly apart, but this time keep moving them and you will notice that, the further they are apart, the weaker the energy will feel. Keep moving them apart until you can barely feel the breeze between your hands. Your hands will begin to shake when you reach the end; this is because you are about to break the connection you have made with the energy. Once you have stopped moving your hands, the distance between them is the size of your aura at this moment.

Another technique is to keep your dominant hand still while moving the other to a horizontal position and pointing those fingers two centimetres towards the dominant palm. Slowly move the horizontal hand up and down, and you will notice a slight tingle in the other hand where the fingers are pointing. This is because you are shooting your energy through the fingers and onto the receiving hand. When you move the other hand further away and bring it in closer, the tingling sensation will feel stronger, almost like a soft stabbing pain.

Keep in mind that, if you practise with someone else, they will also feel the tingling sensation as you work with them. Having someone else to validate it can aid in the process of learning to touch this energy.

Are these forces good or evil?

black	for yourself
white	universal

With magik we manipulate energy. It is the design of our willpower that makes this magik good or evil. It also depends on where you are calling the energy from. Defining one type of energy as good or evil will distort its true meaning. When you channel energy, how you direct it and for what purpose you are using the energy are what defines it as good or evil. It is impossible to summon a pure source of light without the contrast of evil. By understanding that these energies can also be destructive, you can channel a higher vibration.

When you start to sense, see and touch these energies, the next logical step is to learn how to interpret what you are seeing. As you gaze upon an individual, you will see colours emerge around them, and in certain spots on their aura you will come to notice changes. Various other colours and energy patterns will become evident.

By now you should have grasped the meanings of the different colours. But when relating that information to the body, these meanings do not full describe or explain why the colours are located where they are in someone's aura. With an auric field, the colours and their locations can change these meanings. To explain this I need to make reference to the "chakras," the energy centres of the physical body, each governed by a specific colour. Once you are able to conflate the meanings of colours with those of the chakras, you will get a better understanding of what you are seeing.

The chakras

Chakra means "wheel of light" and chakras are circular spirals of moving energy. They are commonly referred to as the seven lotuses of life, for they cover every region of the body and, like the lotus, they open and close. There are seven basic energy centres of the body, each of which governs a part of both the physical and spiritual body.

The first chakra is located on top of the skull and is called the crown chakra; this is the point where energy enters the body. The second is located above the eyebrows in the centre of the forehead and is called the third-eye chakra, the centre of your psychic potential.

The third chakra is located near the voice box and is called the throat chakra; this is where you express yourself, the point of inspiration. The fourth is located above your heart and is naturally called the heart chakra. This is where the energy from the throat chakra continues and grows, the point that relates to nurturing, love and personal growth.

The fifth chakra is located above the navel, close to the stomach, and is called the solar plexus; this is the physical centre of the body. It is where everything enters and is interpreted, where we deal with our day-to-day problems, illnesses and emotions.

The sixth is located below the navel in the lower abdomen and is called the sacral (sexual) chakra. It is the centre of sexual energy and desire, the ego and the way we see ourselves from another's point of view: our self-esteem and self-worth.

The seventh chakra is located at the base and is known as the root chakra. It represents the physical world; working alongside the sacral chakra, the root chakra is the humanity and survival urge inside us.

To follow is a diagram that gives an overview of the human body and the position of each energy centre, what you now know as the chakras.

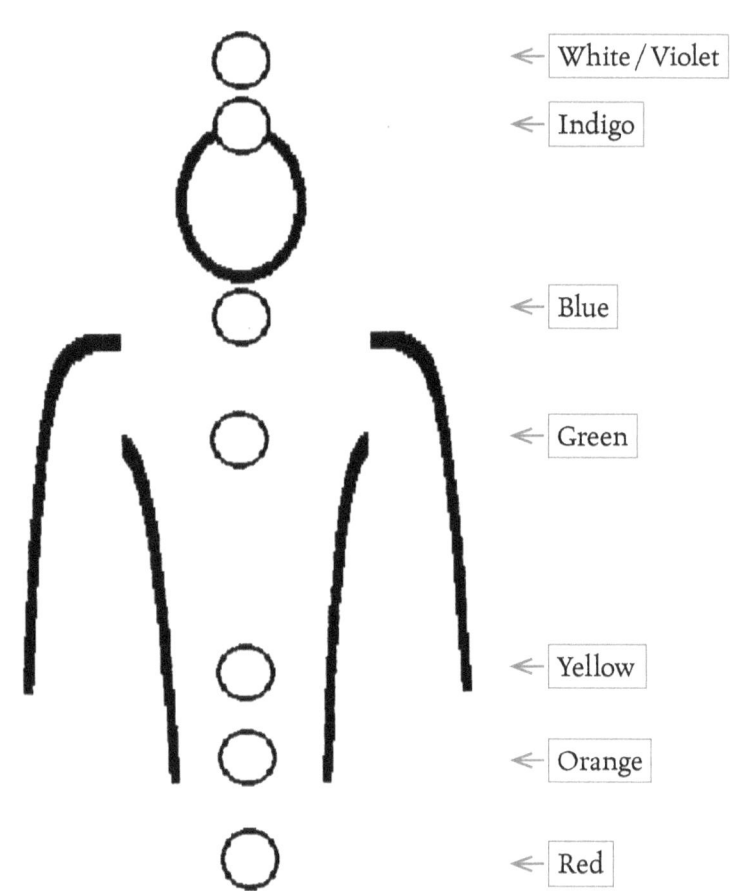

Chapter 7

Power of healing

We search throughout our lives for the answers to questions we are not even sure of, and for the meaning of our existence in this life. Working with energy and the hidden nature of true magik will open up doors you didn't even know you were knocking on, because what we are looking for is all around us and within our grasp. We search for emotional fulfillment. That career you pursued unsuccessfully or relationship that fell apart left you feeling empty, as if you wanted something more out of life. Whenever we feel down, alone or unfulfilled, the main complaint is lack of energy, the will to carry on. The same goes for anything else where your heart isn't in it because you are not inspired and challenged to use both your creative and mental capabilities.

This is where working with healing energies comes in: it is a process of combining your own energy with that of the universe in order to heal. Imagine you are faced with a situation where you would usually lose motivation, and picture yourself with an infinite supply of energy at your disposal. Instead of feeling unfulfilled, you are lifted out of your current energy level to a higher level of being where you can continue your daily routine without noticing all the negative aspects you would normally have dwelled on. When working with energy in the practice of magik, you do not need to harness the full potential of its power in order to achieve your goals, nor do you use the same techniques for magik as you use for other energy work such as healing.

In magik you invoke and control all types of energy to fuel your rituals, but in a healing you only channel energy, and the energy is that of the universe and, in Wicca, the God and Goddess. To give a better understanding, I have included here both a ritual for healing and a technique for channelling the healing energies of the universe.

The first is a spell that involves the combined use of your own will and the energy that dwells within nature, in this case water because of its healing properties. The spell is to be done on a Sunday night while the moon is full, preferably under or near running water. Before you begin the ritual, take a cleansing bath to which you add 1 drop of sandalwood, 1 drop of lavender and 3 drops of rosemary, and then call upon the Goddess to infuse it with healing energy. Once you have bathed, thank the Goddess for her assistance.

Healing waterfalls

He/she travelled, across the land
Not able to walk or even stand.
Through the blue rainforest
Beyond the blue mountains
Into the blue waterfall.
Drop by drop, as the blue water falls
So to does the pain and aches ALL!
Until he/she is standing bright blue
So did the healing come to you
Walk with the Goddess and be true
The healing has come to (recipient)
Surrounding him/her in blue.

While the water is running over you, picture the pain or injury being washed away, then say:

Pain wash away, restoring his/her strength
His/her health, his/her freedom to move
So (recipient) may again (desired outcome)
So mote it be!

The second technique involves the channelling of universal energy, sometimes referred to as unconditional love. I have already mentioned briefly the use of unconditional love; when you channel such energy through you, no words can describe the pure delight and uplifting sensations you receive. It feels as if one voice, one being made of all that is light wraps its celestial arms around you and sends you the warmest, most unconditional love of understanding and passion you will ever know.

The art of channelling

The main principle to remember is that you are not drawing off your own power or energy; in fact, all you are is a divine instrument, a tool through which you channel universal/spirit-like energies. Find yourself a quiet place where you can concentrate away from the mundane distractions of life and centre your being. Add to the atmosphere a few candles and incense. You'll find that, as night approaches, your own awareness grows; knowing this will enable you to explore which hour of the day best suits this and other rituals you undertake. The room now set up and the curtains drawn, light the candles and incense. It is not necessary to place any protection on this sacred place. Sit down comfortably and set your thoughts free, making sure there is no fear at play. While you drift into a meditative state, remember your breathing: as with any meditation, rhythmic breathing will enable you to maintain the energy flow once the gates have opened and you begin to function as a channel of light.

Firstly picture nothing, be nothing; all you have to do at this stage is raise your own energy high enough to prohibit thoughts from flowing in uncontrollably. In time it will be possible to channel messages as well as the energy from spirits/universal beings. Once you are at a comfortable level, proceed by visualising yourself as a being of light. Raise your awareness even higher and shift your consciousness far beyond the physical realm. In the back of your mind, hold onto the image of yourself that "you are energy, you sense only energy" then, almost simultaneously, you become what you have willed. Direct your light towards the universe and tap into its energy, remembering that you are now part of this divine light; visualise the energy travelling through the celestial cord you have created between the universe and yourself. The energy soars through your crown into the room, filling it with light, then shooting up through the clouds and into the universe. At the moment you pierce the universe, its energy flows towards you; feel this energy surge through your body and into your hands, which you now place upon the client. Trust your intuition, your inner voice, for the universal energies will guide your hands.

Directing the healing energy from the universe through yourself and into the client's body without draining your own energy may seem difficult at first, but once you can identify the feeling of absolution from the energy flowing through you, mastering this technique will become easier. When performing a healing in this manner, your own energy will be amplified and you will feel a slight tingling/burning sensation in your hands. Perseverance is the key because, when you achieve this level of healing regularly, you will be able to channel the universal energies at will. Be sure to rid the client of any negative energy by sweeping your hands over their body, and also cleanse yourself by rinsing your hands in water to discard any of the client's energy that may have attached itself to you.

Reiki on the other hand, which is not bound by any faith, is an eastern biofield therapy for channelling energies to promote recovery, reduce stress and pain messages. The healing, if you prefer, takes place on an individual level and, unlike other healing modalities, reiki works as a support therapy, amplifying energy and enabling the body to recover. In a clinical setting, practitioners are able to transmit electric impulse signals through their palms, either hands-on or a few centimetres above the skin, so the client feels a sensation ranging from extreme heat to a slight tingling. I am not about to teach you this age-old technique, as there are several attunements needed to render you capable of practising, but do encourage you to discover what is the best technique for you. I work with several modalities, but my passion lies in calling for the aid of spirit and using seichim, which you could call the Egyptian equivalent of reiki.

Here are three charts that will enable you to understand further the art of healing. Whether you use the method of sympathetic magik, your own energy or the channelling of some outside force, these charts will educate you further on the visualisation of symbols while influencing an outcome, and an expansion of hands-on healing, including the locations where the hands are to be placed.

Runes

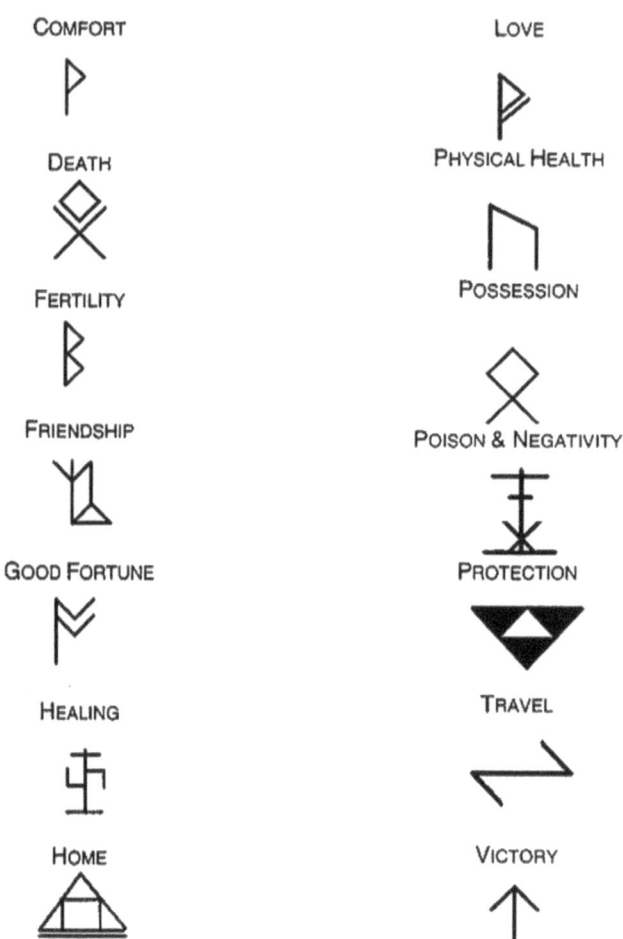

Reiki

AMPLIFICATION

ABSENT HEALING

DISCONNECTION/ RELEASE

EMOTIONS/ RELEASE OF PAIN

FEAR

SPIRITUAL HEALING

PROTECTION

TRUTH

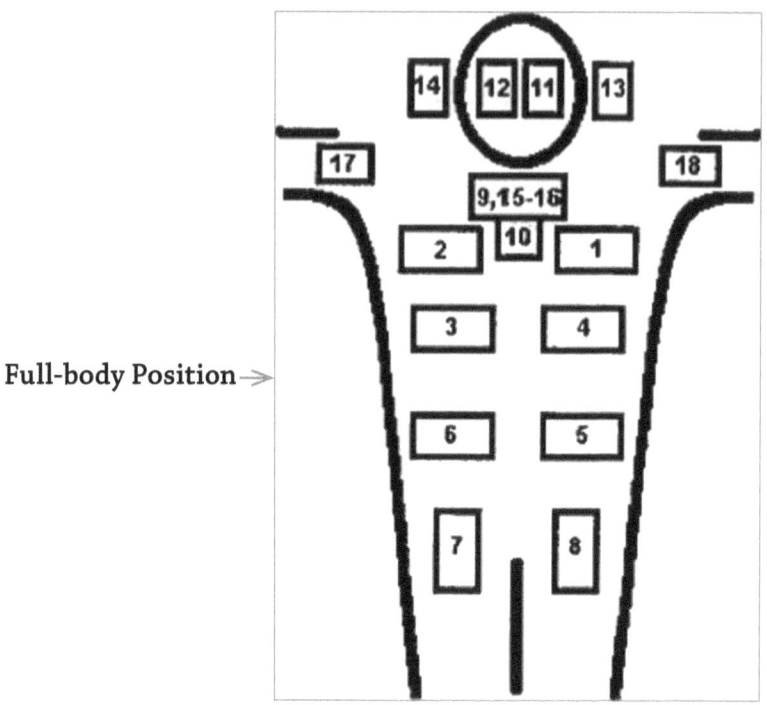

Full-body Position →

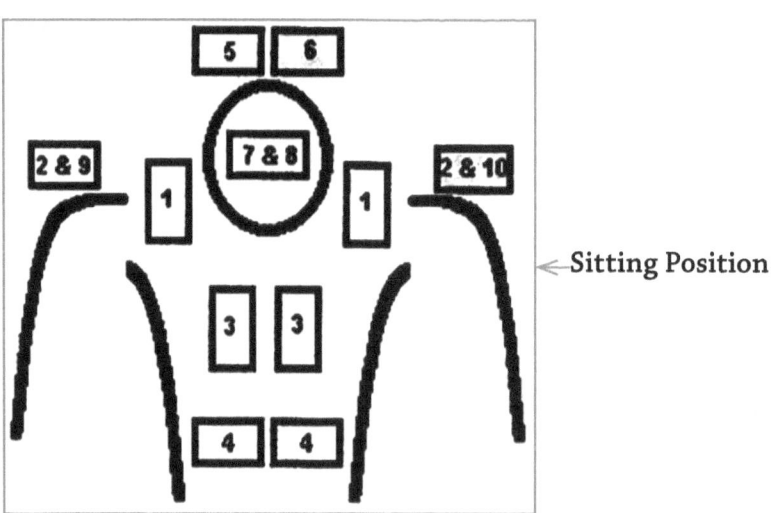

← Sitting Position

When you perform an energy healing, messages may become clear in your mind and are then deciphered and relayed to the client. This happened to me when there was no client, only myself and the power of *seichim*. While receiving my reiki and seichim masters' energy healing during the final attunements and in the days that followed, I received four unique symbols that I had not before seen on the physical plane. Before these images from my third eye escaped my thoughts, I asked my guides to attune them to me; now I use them in all my healing sessions. The channelling of energy and entities is different to receiving messages from spirit that you did not ask for. It is a common trait in human behaviour to push aside such things; we are always asking questions, but when we start receiving answers we tend to shut down and ignore them. Sometimes we take these messages for granted, and dismiss our "little voice" inside or intuition. But if you catch yourself with an unfamiliar thought or feeling, then chances are it is from a foreign entity. Unlike the previous charts, with the four seichim symbols I will give you only the names in which I received them and leave their purpose, their power, up to you. Work with them and you will discover their true potential. What I will tell you is this: the first is a master symbol, a tumble lock.

Seichim – channelled symbols

The key
– *To follow the path you already lead*

Sei har
– *The technical rose*

Cherubim
– *The voice*

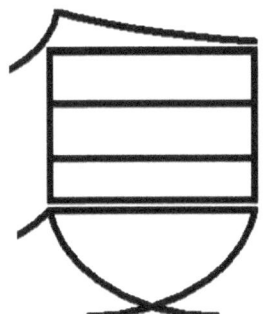

EOH HOH ILM
– *Four sides ... a pyramid*

Colour therapy

The use of colours in healing is not a new concept; in fact, the use of colour therapy has crossed over into the mainstream practice of psychology. There is a common trend in psychiatric clinics towards the inclusion of colour/art therapies as part of their rehabilitation programs, even embracing the notion that colours have always played a part in our moods, and that the way we feel about a particular place, the way we see and show ourselves to society, are positive steps in the recovery process. Wearing the right colour during a ritual has been known to enhance the effect; for example, for a love spell the colour of choice should be red or, in the case of a healing love spell, blue or purple may be more appropriate. In the fields of magik and healing, and in your daily life, colour has an important role. Understanding this and applying them will give a different perspective on how you approach a client for a healing, a ritual you are about to cast, or the style of clothes you wear.

The colours and their meanings are listed in Appendix B. Here are a few simple techniques in relation to using colours and their corresponding formulas in your magik and, most importantly, in healing.

Absent healing

You need a picture of the person who requires the healing and some coloured markers. It is best to use a full-body photograph that shows only the individual you are to heal. Take a marker and draw a circle around the person. At this point direct all your healing energies into the colour, while picturing that it has begun to merge with their body. Now take up another marker and draw a circle around the problem area of this person, then visualise the energy targeting this area and also engulfing the person. The colours used should be pink and blue, although any healing colours will do. Using this technique in the same manner for protection will work just as effectively; the colour black is the most suitable in this case.

Centre of light

The chakras are the body's main energy centres. To clearly understand the need to clear/ heal them, we only need to look at the human body as a system of energy: within this system, the chakras are the wheels that make it run, and the aura is an outer layer which protects and reflects that system. When there is a blockage, an imbalance in this network of energy, an individual's vital life force will weaken, meaning the auric field has lowered to a vibration that leaves the body open to "dis-ease" where the body is not at ease, not at peace with itself. A basic technique for clearing the chakras is to place a crystal on each chakra and let the healing power of the crystals cleanse them. The method I use involves candles and the magik of light. When you are performing this ritual, take care as you run the candle over the chakra points. To prevent wax from dripping onto the body, cut a piece of paper into a circle and make a small hole in the centre, then slide the paper halfway down the candle to catch any wax that may drip. After you light the candle, begin to move it along the chakras. As you reach each point, stop and visualise a shaft of pure light entering and filling the body. Once you have finished, hold this sensation of light within you for a brief moment, then take the candle and let it finish burning on your altar.

Charged waters

You can find coloured bottles in any discount outlet, or you can wrap clear bottles in coloured cellophane. It is best to try and collect several different-sized bottles in a variety of colours, so you can experiment and find which bottle works best. Take the coloured bottles and fill them with water. As with the above technique, this one incorporates the use of charging. Once you have filled all of them to the top, replace the lids and seal them tightly, then put them separately on a window sill during the day. Over a week the sun will shine through the bottles enough to charge them with their actual colours. Within two weeks you will have several bottles that can aid in the healing process, and you may even use them when working magik. Infuse a bottle that is charged with the energy, and this can enhance the spell you are working on.

Healer's curtain

An hour before you perform a healing, place a thin sheet over the window and the light from outside will shine through the rays of healing light you have chosen. Be sure to place the healing table in direct contact with that light. To better aid the healing you could also cover the healing table with the same sheet moments before you start your healing session.

Healing bottle brew

To a saucepan add four teaspoons of vinegar and four teaspoons of honey, then heat the two until they form a single liquid. Add four cups of water and bring to a boil. Remove it from the flame, add twelve sunflower seeds, and leave the brew to simmer for five minutes. Once cooled, pour it into a clear bottle and seal. Leave it on a window sill, preferably at night when there is a full moon so that it will charge the potion; the next day, wake up and meditate with the bottle in hand. Visualise your energy going into the bottle, then remove the sunflower seeds and bury them, the ritual now being completed. Store the bottle out of sunlight and, when you need the healing properties in this brew, a few sips is all you need.

Meditation

Visualisation is the key to any healing. Whether you need to be grounded or just need additional energy, wrap yourself in a green blanket and meditate on the colour you are using. As with all methods of colour therapy, the colour should change as need dictates.

Talisman

This is easy to make: all you require is a brown cord (the size may vary) and a small coloured disc, whether crafted then painted or simply cut out of cardboard. Once you have gathered these two items, inscribe the disc with the runic symbol for healing, then tie it to the centre of the cord. Tie the talisman around the injury, place the talisman on the problem area, wear it around the neck or just carry it until the healing is complete.

Temple walls

If you have dedicated a room for the purpose of performing magik and casting circles, attention should be focused on the temple walls. They can change the energy within the room. The most practical colours to use relating to the cardinal points are green, yellow, red and blue. Another popular choice would be to use earth tones as a tribute to the God and Goddess. It is your place of worship and the colours you choose should reflect that. If the main focus is spirituality and healing, then either a pale blue or deep purple would apply; if it is life you wish to bring to your temple, then I would suggest warm colours like orange or yellow. The atmosphere within those walls is as important as the rituals performed; black, for instance, refers to the raising of energy and the night, and is an ideal colour to use in the temple.

Similar to the Healing waterfall ritual, what follows are several techniques that involve the use of the written word and the process of visualisation in your healing. You will learn more later when you delve further into the realms of empowering and creating and performing magik. The first technique is designed to heal emotional pain. When we are emotionally scarred by an event, we tend to shut down and avoid getting close again. These words were created in understanding of this, to create a process of consciously accepting change and opening up the soul to life again without fear of the consequences. Love will find you whether or not you are ready; it is your choice whether to take that chance, for you will not always be the victim of cruel circumstance.

Injured Butterfly – To heal emotional pain

It is time to summon the butterfly again
To spread their wings and fly
Cocoon spun all around me
I no longer wish to hide.
Through thoughts and fears
My life has formed
I open up the door again
To my heart I can no longer defend.
I stand here unsure of life
This is what I ask
Be a butterfly once more
To bring my love at last.
Broken hearts and shattered dreams
I've built a wall between
I can't hide from pain
My heart must beat again!

Aradia's potion

Aradia has always been known in Wicca. This potion allows you to use both the healing properties of the oils and at the same time tap into her beautiful energy. This spell was given to me by Melissa who often delves into the realm of healing; she wishes to convey that the oils can be altered to perfect the scent you require, so refer to Appendix D (Aromatherapy oils) if you would prefer to add another oil. The key oils to use are eucalyptus, juniper, niaouli and palmarosa. You will need to acquire a small spraybottle and an eyedropper for each oil to aid in the mixing process. Begin by adding 1 drop of juniper, 3 drops of palmarosa, 2 drops of niaouli and 5 drops of eucalyptus. Mix and stir, seal and say:

I hereby call the Goddess Aradia
Send me your healing power

To assist me in making this enchanted potion
Immersed in the oils shall they heal
Aid in my health, to Aradia I kneel.
Apply potion, then say:
Aradia's energies are within me
Helping me heal!
I thank her for these powers each day
By using this oil
All ills fade away.
Around and behind
Healing light surrounds
Oils I thank. Help me they must!
Lifting my health to greater strength.

Blessing evil

I send you love.
Not a curse!
Yes, you harmed me
I am not like you
That I love, not worse.
Uplift your soul.
Encircle the mind
Erase the evil.
Hatred and despise
You will no longer find.
No more tears
I lend to you
Love is sent, harm not again
I believe in your soul
The true self I now mend!
Shall the kindness I show
My courage and good nature

Be your reward, know this
Love comes not only from me
But from the merciful Goddess
So mote it be!

Padded walls – to fight depression
Ritual to Isis:

Confined in my thoughts
Reach out, cannot
Be but me!
I turn to Isis
Sow me a dress, laced in tears
Hopefully then ...
My pain will disappear.
Isis, queen of all this!
I am absent, confused at best
Cast your magik, spread your tears
Heal my mind and the heart
Shall you remain with me
Through what's to come
Within me, that's dark!
So mote it be.

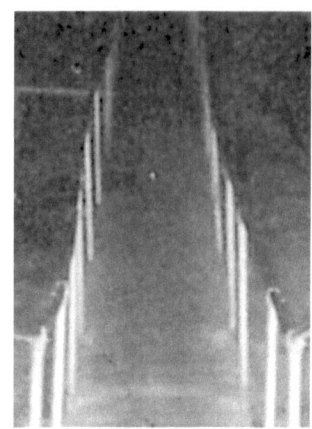

Soul deep

>Jagged blade upon the soil,
>Twist and turn the thoughts in deep.
>I catch them solid!
>Before rain washes my presence from you.
>Know not that I was there …
>This spell be cast upon (recipient) whom would be unfair.
>A penny for your thoughts.
>Curtain be drawn,
>See in your mind, through any brick walls,
>(recipient)'s truths shall I find!
>Permission I must seek,
>To enter your darkest cloud
>Permission granted upon your sins,
>Consciously unaware that you had let me in.
>I now can cast! I now can sow!
>With all knowledge of you, I now know!
>Blade remove, hole be sown.
>For a penny I leave, buried in your mind.
>Reflect and mirror, what your soul needs to find!

The next technique has been described earlier in regards to the reading of energy fields such as auras. The principle remains the same, although with this ritual you are channelling divine light into yourself instead of another. You can either use it for a healing or to empower yourself with the purest energy.

Shaft of light
I light a candle.
Stands, altar tall
Bring light unto this day
Run the water to it, I fall!
Drown the night away
To all ills, ye must fade.
Under, water walls.
Send your healing light
Fill me up, toe to breast.
Emerge the gift of sight.
Vision of truth.
Names unsaid!
I thank the Lord,
For my mind read.
Water off, stands me.
To Lady I thank in prayer
For this flame, water's burn.
Sent you love did I you!
I bless the footsteps.
Lord and Lady of me knew.

Say it once and the door shall open

Say it times three and we shall see

Say it by nine and it shall be mine!

That is the way of the mantra.

Ethean

Part III

Putting magik into practice

Chapter 8

Ritual craft

If you are unable to find a particular spell or ritual, and are searching for what is missing in your magik practices, then creating your own ritual is the next step in your journey. You can empower the rituals you already have, or take a new direction and start your own. Original spells and rituals were not created to appeal to a mainstream audience; they were formed for only those within a particular coven to perform, and so were designed to suit the beliefs of those members. Diversity permeates the vast stream of religious beliefs that form what we know as Wicca. There can be no key book of shadows which holds all rituals and spells, because there is more then one tradition of Wicca; to name a few: Gardnerian, folk, Celtic, forest and angel. Each has its own set of beliefs, yet the structure of their faith is relatively the same, which means you can either adapt their rituals or create your own using their principles. The structure behind a ritual is not fixed, for everyone has his or her own style, but I can give you the basic components of creating your own ritual. Not all the eight key points that are listed below apply to every type of ritual or spell; they are included so that you can use it as a checklist of all the possible components, in order to perfect your own design.

The eight basic components of a ritual/spell:
- purpose/goal
- materials

- timing
- breathing technique
- invocation
- purification
- the circle
- raising/earthing power

Apply these components where necessary because, as you may know, raising power and casting a circle do not apply to any traditional spell, and the same goes for a ritual: you will not always require the assistance of an entity or need to use materials. To better understand each key principle, I have also included a guide to questions that you may have. Learn all you can about the process of creating your own rituals/spells and watch as your magik grows.

Purpose/goal

Clarify what is to be achieved. If you are to cast a spell for success, you must make it clear what are you want to succeed in: is it a promotion you seek or new employment? Is it exams you wish to pass or advancement to the next year level? Answering these questions will enable the spell to work in the right direction.

Materials

Performing a ritual in a cave off the seashore at the stroke of midnight, with candles lit and incense rising high, is a little melodramatic when all you desire is prosperity. The importance of the spell is what you put into it, not the grand performance of a ritual. All you need is the magikal words and a few candles, oils, maybe even a feather. It depends on the purpose of the spell and what kind of materials you wish to use (if any) to symbolise and enhance the ritual. See the appendices at the back of this book.

Timing

The phases of the moon and the days of the week govern what type of magik we should perform, in accordance with the information given in the previous section, *Moon phases*, and the following list.

Monday:	dreams, intuition, psychic powers and femininity
Tuesday:	war, enemies, conflict, masculinity and courage
Wednesday:	fear, communication, travel and the arts
Thursday:	career, finance, law, desire and prosperity
Friday:	love, friendship, passion, beauty and nature
Saturday:	building, protection, karma and negativity
Sunday:	hope, success, money, ambition and healing

Breathing technique

The method of breathing is critical when performing high magik, because the right breathing places you in a relaxed state and balances the energy centres of the body, so that you are able to separate from the conscious mind and enter an altered state. The technique that I use is very simple:

Inhale for six seconds, then hold for a brief moment. Exhale for six.

Invocation

This is a term commonly used in Wicca to mean calling the God and Goddess, to either watch over the circle while you perform a ritual or assist you in the working of magik or a healing.

Purification

Before you partake in magik, you may wish to devise a small cleansing ritual to rid yourself of negativity and discard any dead energy that is attached to you. For example, taking a purifying bath with oils and candles, or rinsing your hands in rosewater; the choice is yours.

The circle

The circle is the best place to perform magik, because it protects those within its walls of light and can aid in raising power. It is not necessary to cast a circle for each ritual. All you need to determine is whether both the presence of a deity and the advantages of a circle are needed.

Raising/earthing power

Raising power during a ritual can be done by increasing your personal power through techniques such as meditation or through the use of an entity, empowered objects or any form of folk magik. When reaching the end of a spell, always earth the remaining energy that has been built up, and remember to thank as well as dismiss any entity that you have summoned.

Creating a new spell or ritual can be even more exciting than performing one. Personalise it with your own style and infuse it with your love, making it an extension of your magikal self. When performing your own magik, you will speak the words with greater depth and understanding, taking your awareness to the next evolutionary level of life.

Chapter 9

Psychic protection

Placing a barrier between yourself and evil might seem overcautious and unnecessary, but if all you are doing is preventing negativity from being sent your way, then there is no reason not to put these psychic barriers up. There are many techniques for psychic self-defence, ranging from simple visualisation to advanced rituals and spiritual methods. The most common method of psychic protection is the use of an affirmation, because this not only works to calm your nerves and create a positive atmosphere, but also sends out the message that you are protected. Try using the one of the affirmations below next time you feel fearful or believe evil has been sent your way, and see the difference.

Affirmations for psychic protection

- Goddess walketh with me, surround me in your love.
- Spheres of gold rightly cast, protect me now.
- Michael! Spread your wings and fly.
- Protect me until the evil passes by.
- I walk within a circle of divine light.
- Nothing shall enter.
- Darkness of the night, shroud me out of sight.
- Spirit guides protect me now, as I will it shall be.

Visualisation still plays a small part when reciting an affirmation; as with working magik, you must see a pleasant outcome to your situation. When another person asks you to assist them with psychic protection, you can use the same affirmations but instead visualise them upon the other person, for example, "I cast a sphere of golden light around her, protect her now." Other helpful visualisations are set out below; remember that your thoughts have the power to cause change, so use that to your advantage.

Visualisation techniques for psychic protection

- To protect the home draw a pentagram over the doors and windows.
- Picture a guard dog in front of the main entrance door and if possible ensure that all outside gates are closed, as an open gate invites negativity.
- Surround your home or vehicle with a gold/pink sphere.
- Take your awareness out of the present and into a peaceful astral state.
- Send unconditional love to whoever is sending you negativity. This in effect should cause them to stop by appealing to their higher self.
- Doors represents the doorway between worlds. When you wish to rid yourself of negativity, picture a door closing. If you sense unwanted entities in the home, slam a door shut and they will leave immediately.

Protection rituals

Since the term 'protection' applies to many different areas, not all affirmation and visualisation techniques you attempt to use will work. That is why I have included several rituals for protection that can be easily memorised and performed. There are spells to protect you before evil arises, and rituals for when it is too late. Work with them to determine which one suits you best; not all rituals will appeal to you at first, but the ones that do will form a greater connection with you.

Auric vampires

River eyes apart and beyond
Blameless souls reverse across
Fought on thy behalf.
Children of coils in a name
Give breath to me.
Secreted in shadow.
Without hindrance and praise
Only within me.
I am blessed with high magik
Open who art and see!
Who is this?
Entered as a falcon
Gone forth a phoenix
Hail to thee. Afraid of nought!
I know. Guard me not!
River unlock, awaken and part.
Good mornings on this day
To east I will praise.
To the west is he
Thank thee and abide
Honour and command
As I wilt, here as I stand!

Banishment of evil

Take this evil from my sight,
My will alone is my might!
For love I send,

By light I am in
I send away the evil,
He/she did bring.
By harm to none,
So blessed be
The evil that was returned to he/she
As I will it, so mote it be!

Place a black candle in the centre of your altar. While focusing on the candle, meditate on the evil being reflected (bounced) back by your will alone. Your burning desire!

Bast storm

By blood and cloud I cast a storm
Rain from my hell to his/hers now below
Shalt receive what so harshly sent
Gracious Bast, rid me of pain!
To him/her feel my suffering over again.
Walk not, heart 'tis bleeds
I release this curse
NOW fall on your knees.

Bewitchment

By the Maiden, Mother and Crone
Lend me your power,
To do as I desire
Undo this bewitched!
Undo this bewitched!
To heal what has been done
By the power of sisters three
Send your healing onto me.

Consecration of evil

> Through the candle burning bright
> Let the misfortune and evil be set alight
> By the blazing light of the flame
> Be gone, harm not me again!

Draw a picture of what is troubling you or write a note describing the circumstances, then place this into a fireproof container. While you are burning a tall gold candle, repeat the spell until the picture or note has completely burnt. Dispose of the ashes immediately, away from the home, then walk away not looking back.

Cooling-off spell

You will need a plastic container big enough to place a photo in, with a depth of 2 to 5 centimetres. Half-fill the container and place a photo of the person who needs to cool off gently in the water, face down, making sure it stays afloat. If you don't have a photo, draw an image of the person or use a piece of paper with their name on it. Place the container in the freezer and say:

> I put to rest
> Your wicked ways
> Banishing your negativity
> To all I do lay.

Wait until the water has frozen and then remove the container from the freezer. Carefully remove any ice that may have formed on the back of the photo or note, and then dry it. Now inscribe on the back of the paper your intentions (i.e. for them to cool off) and place it back into the container. Then fill the remaining half of the container and place it back into the freezer. This time, before closing the door say:

> I seal the evil at hand. Cool off!
> To you (recipient) I command.

Close the freezer door immediately after these words, then leave the container until it has frozen or for as long as you believe it will take for the recipient to cool off.

Cradle me

A lucky charm is what this is ...

A little pouch is to be lined with cinnamon, cypress and bergamot and part of a lotus plant which is torn. Add a single hair from the person the charm is for and 3 teardrops from you to bind the spell. A special something I also like to add is a drop of lavender to calm the nerves. Once the pouch is complete, these are the words to cast upon it:

I tie, I mend
I lose, I gain
What can now happen!
When all you see is this pain.
Carry me through
What it be ...
Carry this charm
Lucky me!

Dead energy

Dragons are beautiful creatures to use in magik, and this is one of my favourite methods of dispelling unwanted energies. Visualise that a cloud of grey is swirling up covering your entire body then, as fast as it climbed, it drops. During this exercise picture yourself shaking off all flakes of negativity.

Divine rays – protection for self and home

In extreme circumstances you may take a course of action that you otherwise would not take if you had the chance to think before committing an act of hatred. This ritual has been created for such a situation, when great danger is approaching, and when your only choice is to either take up a course of action you will later regret, or put your life in the hands of spirit. I give you the option of taking the path of light, rather than the destructive path of hatred you may be inclined to take if desperation gets hold of you. I am not suggesting that you do not call the authorities, but what should you do while you wait for them to come? What can you do if they arrive too late? With all your magikal training and beliefs, you know that your wellbeing comes before one who would harm you. Try to shift your awareness away from your surroundings and draw off your emotions, letting the tears fuel the fire in your heart, and then say:

Ancient spirits of old, unite before me now
Three rays from the spectrum of light
Each a shaft of divine love.
Sisters of thy warrior's might!
Ishtar, Babylonian creator-goddess, arrive! Arrive!!
Cut through his/her soul,
Destroy his/her strength
Send him/her away from me at any length!
By ray of two, arrive to me! Arrive!!
Sukhemel, Egyptian lion-goddess.
Shine your divine ray through his/her eyes
Blind him/ her from me,
Shalt he/she never harm
Leave my presence now, in fear you flee!
To the third ye arrive, at the right time.
Hecate, Pagan warrior-goddess
Blind and bound, unable to move.
Unmask thy evil that is in this man/woman
Shalt he/she be shown true fear,
In his/her own home!
By three sisters combined.
All joint by the spectrum of light
Destroy this man's/woman's will.

Send him/her out of my sight!
By goddesses three.
Bind him/her from harm.
Destroy his/her strength.
Send him/her away, this is what I demand.
If he/she shalt continue, I give the order!
In the black of night
I take his/her will, I take his/her life.
By the goddesses three
Force him/her far away from me!
I give you control of him/her
Do as you wilt. I give the order!
Protect, with no harm to me, no evil be sent back
Destroy this man/woman,
This is what I command!
I leave his/her fate,
His/her will
In thy warriors' hands.
So mote it be!

Enough rope

TIE your lies together!
TRY to deceive the truth!
Knot by knot it tightens
But only a breath away
In time,
Your knots encircle those lives.
Stirring and brewing them together
PULL ... GIVE ENOUGH ...
For you to see!
THREE more steps and you shall fall
TWO more lies and you will know

That I have enough rope
To see through your games.
ONE last step and it be the end
You are hanged
With lies and deceit
Your will, I now defeat.

Escaping fear – to bind an attacker

With each breath you take, I bind thee!
With each thought you make, I bind thee!
With each bone you break
With each poor soul you forsake, I bind thee!
Not able to move or even stand
I take the blood that runs through this man
Not able to harm or to cause a tear
All your strength will now disappear!

Frozen fear

These blocks are made of ice, night falls swiftly
Darkened streets paved in fear and more
Ice stand strong and when you melt
Wash away the evil about.
Tsunami, flood from my heart
Ice-cold daggers! I walk above the street
In cold blocks at night
To all ill, my will defeat.

In threes – to remove nightmares from children

Three big breaths I take with you …
The first being your life
The second being your love
The third being your soul

Three breaths which are yours to the day you grow old
In this moment and the space between
I shall take these with you
So you may dream.
All nightmares and evil I take
Nothing but bliss and joy you seek
This is what I give!
This spell shall not break.
Until you sleep sound
Breathe one, two and three
Do all this without the need
Do all this for yourself without me to lead.
Three big breaths I give to thee ...
Three big breaths, so mote it be.

Lighthouse – all-purpose bewitchment

I cast a storm off me/(recipient)
Clouds recede and tides roll back
Bind its fury, halt its charm.
Send it to he/she who would send me/(recipient) harm!
Mistress of the moon
Shroud me/(recipient) in black
Goddess Hecate
Enchant me/(recipient) you must!
Send all evil to return on wings it came
Disclose not my presence
To him/her whom you now will tame.
Through love,
To him/her I bind
In light, I strip thee of thy strength
No more magik shall he/she find!
Naked of power, so love I send

In a message from the Goddess
Farewell, child!
To thyself you now defend.

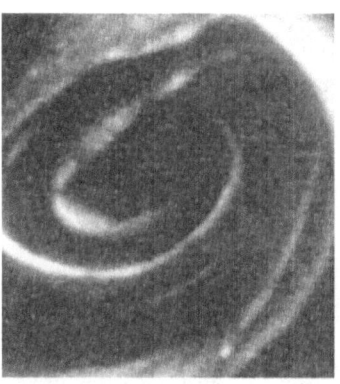

Magik shield

Whatever he/she has cast!
Temple walls cannot contain
My circle has broken
His/her magik causes this pain.
I touch,
Your strength you not give
Love fill! Rid me of this magik
I will not cast his/her unknown evil.

Mental wall

Similar to "Escaping fear," this spell is intended to stop an unfortunate event from occurring. Easy to remember, it will give you confidence to say the words without any trouble remembering a lengthy incantation, as well as creating safe passage for yourself.

Wall of light I now surround
To these (number of people)
Souls I then bound.

Painful tears – send back negativity

By the guardians! (recipient's name)
Receive back the harm you sent/caused
For if one tear is shed, it shall put a bounty on your head
If two tears shall fall, I am not responsible for it at all
If the third tear comes, karma's work will be done!
By the god of protection, bring forth thy power
By will of mine, shall it happen three times
By the power of three times three, so mote it be!

Protection-jar ritual

Assemble all the following ingredients on your altar, leaving aside the needle and blood, mirror dust, and the water and soil. You will add these later in the ritual. First place the remaining ingredients into the jar, ensuring that the handkerchief is situated approximately in the centre.

- a small jar with a screw-on lid (to seal the ingredients)
- a white handkerchief stained with tears (to affirm the need)
- a handful of brass screws (to ward off evil)
- a personal object made of gold (for protection of spirit)
- a broken mirror, separated into two groups:
    - broken pieces (for protection)
    - mirror dust (for luck)
- a new sewing needle (for creation)
- three drops of blood (for connection)
- half a cup of water and a small handful of loose soil (for protection of the jar)

Place the lid upside-down on the jar with the mirror dust on top. When the moon is full and high in the sky, add the dust to the jar and say:

Moon twilight
Reflect above and below

Combine the ingredients
Like a well-made ball of snow.

Pick up the needle and prick your finger to add three drops of your blood* to the jar, and then the needle. As it combines with the sharp objects, it forms a connection to you; feel this as it starts the protection, then say:

I prick my finger
So it may bleed.
Three drops of blood
I add to protect thee.

You are confirming that this is a voluntary act, not to harm yourself but to protect, and that strengthens the potency of the magik. If the weather is clear, leave your altar and proceed outside to perform the rest of the ritual. Choose a spot where the moon is in sight, then shout aloud:

By blood and snow
I mix and stir
In dead of night
I now can seal this rite!

Without delay, seal the jar tight! While picturing a golden light around you, say:

I cast a circle of protection
Around my life!
For if the jar remains unscathed
The protection will last forever until that day!

The protection will remain until the jar is damaged. It is best to bury the jar to guarantee a considerable length of protection. If the jar is found by someone, what will stop them from using the stored magik against you? The water and soil are used to wash away the magik created and ground any energies that may be left behind within the jar. In a final effort to protect yourself.

*The use of blood magik is always optional; refer to Chapter 6: Energy Types.

Restrain anger

    Bring it now, not then
    No more dramas, no more chaos
    Listen to me (recipient) this is
    At an end, what is?
    Not to say!
    I force you to do it my way.
    Kneel and repent
    Don't cause an evil you don't regret
    Forget her/him …
    This is NOW your karmic debt
    I (name) cast in sorrow
    No more worries come tomorrow
    As I wilt, so mote it be.

The need and desire for protection will always dominate the strength of the ritual you are working with. Infuse as much energy and thought into protection as you would into any other form of magik; the more emotions you can put into the ritual, the more fuel you add to the blazing fire that protects you!

Self-destructive behaviour

    Thought to creation
    I cast all of this!
    Take that which I cannot
    Take that which I will not miss.
    Misfortunes and evil at bay
    I cast once more!
    Direct and receive only love …
    Light shall surround me.
    I am strength, I am power
    Karma settle these scores
    In name of the watchtowers

I shall not plead or make a sound
This is my will, my blood
'Tis this then I am bound.
Set again the path that led
Set again my soul
To all evil within,
I put to bed.
Within this I say and set myself free.
As I wilt, so mote it be!

Walk alone

Beating heart,
Bind him/her
Race to tie and bound
Beat his/her force before we meet
Racing heart,
Capture him/her without a sound.

Weak threats

You are weak
As the candle flame
Burn, extinguish
I can blow out.
Receive, not sent
Candle melt your strength
Your negativity,
Not felt
This evil flame in you
I now blow out!

Yellow rose – to keep a secret

Undo what I did
Undo what you know
Keep it a secret …
What no one else should know!
I bind your lips
Erase yours thoughts
Keeping a secret
Is what you will be taught.
Yellow rose watch
As he/she walks about
Protect my secret
Not to wilt or fade in sight
What he/she knows shall die
Or prick him/her you might.
Friendship and honesty
The lines between
In the truth that he/she possesses
Lies the charm to this spell
You put to rest!

Chapter 10

True magik

*Direct influence over our environment,
through the application of our will.*

We are faced with thousands of subtle decisions each day; luckily we have the means of finding answers. In ancient Egypt, magik (*heka*) was said to have been given to humankind to use as a protective weapon against unfortunate events. In an effort to cover the majority of situations you are confronted with, you will find several practical rituals set out here so that you have all the tools needed for the task within the spoken words. You can either perform the ritual as it is written or enhance it through the use of empowerment, which is described in the next chapter.

Be sure to fully understand the term 'empowerment.' Although you can empower a ritual through herbs, incense, oils, candles, etc., using visualisation can be an even more powerful aid in your magikal work if you are able to strengthen and harness its true potential.

From your thoughts to creation,
What you will so mote it be!

Chanting is the most effective form of magik: it not only confirms your purpose, your magikal intent, but it gives the spell direction, which ensures a more accurate outcome. When it's time to perform one of these, remember to repeat the enchanted words at least three to nine times, nine representing the power of three times three in karma.

Anomaly – crystal scrying

Un-cloud my mind, answers to it I find.
Emotions bind, hold me down!
I can't see or hear a sound.
Clouded are my eyes, need see!
I require answers,
Show them to me.

Best friend

A spell I cast on you
Connect us as past
Separate in same
I send you eternal love
That can never fade away.
Not to be found
Not to be loved
But to have and be
Unremarkably special
To your soul I set free.
By my voice I cast
By these words you'll read
No harm and pure bliss
Shall fall upon thee.

Bright star

I wish upon a star bright,
Grant my wish tonight.
You know what I ask, henceforth
No barriers will keep you from completing this task.

Evil not, harm if so
Wish be granted
By the light of day, star bright!
This wish my karma does not pay.

Burning heart

A gift I send to you with love from my heart ...

Gather a tall pink candle, light it and repeat these words; then burn them. Let the smoke send your message of hope.

Ocean lengths,
Your voice 'tis speaks
Free my soul, apart,
Gentle words of love, part
This time I send to you ...
My heart!
True desires, join
Your pure content, join
Lead you to my bed, rejoice!
In happiness that is now mine.

Candle flame – to overcome nerves

Rain drops and waterfalls
Vast oceans
Set out to sea,
Waves of calm come to me.
Cold and still, so pure
Time to relax
Peace and quiet is the cure
Peace and serenity
Love and Light
Extinguish my nerves, out of sight.

Light a candle and when you reach the last line extinguish the candle flame, and this will extinguish your nerves. Never blow out the flame, for that results in blowing out the magik. Always snuff it out with your fingers or a candle snuffer.

The next ritual is to be performed before you go astral travelling, to guarantee safe passage to and from the astral plane. It involves the summoning of an entity and, although the spirit bodies called upon in this book are safe and of good intentions, as with any invocation remember to thank and dismiss the entity after you have finished, for their presence will not disappear easily! While reading through the magik text, as with all the others you will find it contains an underlying ritual within the spoken word. Not only does this ensure protection, but you are invoking an entity that will increase your ability to enter the astral plane.

Celestial pyramid – astral traveller

Set up four votive-sized candles at each cardinal point. Light the candles, then sit in the centre facing the west, for it was believed in ancient Egypt that is where your spirit dwells when you pass from this life. Once relaxed, say:

Greetings to thee, Anubis, whom behold
Now, the mysteries at the gate
I command thee ...
In casting a crystal pyramid around thine Khat
Oh mighty Anubis, to ye power I adore,
Open thy celestial door.
Pyramid of crystal, put into flight
Hail to thee Anubis,
As my Ba sent forth
Unto the gods' domain
Hail to thou risest from thy Khat
To thee pyramid ascended by Anubis!
In not death or by day,
Shalt thy Ba be seest fare in skies
Praise thee in the realm of sleep,
Thus before awake of day
Riseth from Khat, to walk with Ba
To this I command of thee.
Hail ye, Anubis, set thou Ka free
That I mayest seek and find he, thine enemy!
As ascended Sekhem,
So mote it be.

Change

To the cauldron I add the spider's web
Still spun and full
Stir and stir, the fate be past

All wound down like an hourglass.
A pinch of this and a dash of that
Spider's web twist and turn
Remain spun!
The change has now begun.
OR
No more blood spilt
Pain or sorrow
No more troubles
Come tomorrow.

Confrontation

When you bring yourself,
To face this day
All the cards,
To it be laid.
Your eyes can't lie,
What's deep inside
Confront you must,
To him/her you will confide.

Contact me

Needle and the flame
Pierce his/her thoughts
Make him/her contact me again
Needle in the flame
Burn bright and true
Contact me before night is through
Needle be burnt,
So be you
Seek out, so mote it be!
Stick a needle through a yellow candle at thumb's length from

the wick. Light the candle and repeat the chant until the flame has burnt down to the needle; the person you wish to contact you will usually do so before the flame reaches this point, as the needle works to prick their attention, best described as a nagging sensation.

Crone of wisdom – decision making

I call the powers
That lie within
To grow, to strengthen
Find answers to this decision!
To grow, to strengthen
Find answers to this decision!
I invoke thee, Crone
Lend me your magik, giveth me your wisdom
Be with me throughout,
Making this decision!
Be with me throughout,
Making this decision!
Together we stand!
Giveth me answers, to problems I face
I'll make the final decision
Though I need your inspiration.
To the problem,
It will fade, in tears, go away!
To the problem,
It will fade, in tears, go away!
To the decision,
Be made!

The rhythm of the words is important; the words that are repeated play a significant role in the ritual. As you are repeating the magikal text, the tone of your voice must become louder and more determined with each new line.

Daily dedication

Déjà vu,
Let me see
Shall I follow the path I must lead
Coinciding with my destiny.
Send me my teacher, show me my passion
Enlighten my soul
Give me all this!
As my body grows old.
Universe hear my prayers,
Aid me in my vision quest
That I may concur,
All the doubts and fears
Soaring my soul higher, to you I am near
Becoming a light to which you inspire.

Dare to be happy

See the world in colour
Through thick and thin
Goddess, stand with me
In strength, happiness I smile.
Shall the God send me inspiration
Carry and guide as I travel though time
Combined are my faith, bringing colourful love,
This is the true sign!

Dragon mist – the art of invisibility

Magik is not a party trick! You will not "vanish" before people's eyes, for the same principle of secrecy as when practising spellcraft plays a major part. You give your spells power because you believe what is to be done will be so, but if others also know then the outcome will be altered. For this particular rite, strong belief is needed not only in your own magikal ability but also in dragons. Memorise this chant and that will make it easier to concentrate on becoming invisible. The key to this technique is to reach a meditative state of relaxation in which you look ahead, making your self-image fade out of focus to the point that you become invisible to others. While concentrating on your breathing, say:

> Dragon mist
> Rise high and tall
> Encircle around me
> Shrouded from eyes all
> Dragon mist
> Rise high and true
> Shroud me from all
> Until I'm through!

While you are repeating the chant, visualise smoke rising from under your feet until it moves over your head, creating a cocoon. Step out of this cocoon of smoke, looking ahead and making your self-image fade out of focus to the point that you become invisible. The dragon mist surrounded your body and then you stepped through it, causing the mist to shroud your physical shell. You now blend in and can move about. But to announce your presence by sound or thought will cause you to be seen.

Dreams

> Awake from a nightmare,
> Not yours!
> But one mind,
> Many voices, not mine.

Familiar

> Three sisters moved across the land
> A Maiden travelled beneath the sea

Our Mother flew across the sky
The Crone holds my kindred
As they all pass me by.
Sisters three, make it clear
Reveal my familiar
That mine eyes have missed
Before I awake, from visions of thee
Night moves quickly
As my familiar is set free.
Each night I dream,
Of sisters three
I see my familiar, by my side
Its identity shall no longer hide!

Family feud

In a heated dispute there are relationships at stake: those of families, friends and others. When arguments escalate out of control, the values that keep these relationships together become thin and sometimes break. This spell is not to force a union or even to help solve the problem. The most important thing is to go back to basics and remember what brought this relationship together and why is it so important. Is it worth ending something so big over something as insignificant as what the dispute is about?

Heat and passions
Thoughts and lies
Undo the bonds,
Of these family ties.
Bring love and surround in peace
Resolve disputes, release grievances
Unite the pair and combine a family
In not pain or anguish shall they mend!
My will to this family's honour I defend.

Love and loyalty
Thoughts and truth
Restore the bonds,
Of these family ties
To each of them
Love will no longer hide.

Forgiveness

I forgive you
For dying,
Not being here
I forgive myself
For feeling this way,
It doesn't seem to be fair.
I take my heart to this pink candle
On the ledge I stand
What you see in me
I will always be that man/woman!
Rise over the sun
Into your night
I lay my tears,
Out of sight.
I rejoice
In memory of you
Knowing only!
That you love me too.
You did not leave
My heart still feeling you beat
I look forward to the night
When we shall again meet!

Foundation – house hunting

    Prayer to the God and Goddess:
    You wouldn't let me get into trouble
    Place me in financial pain,
    So I trust in you
    Send me to my home
    Where I shall lay my roots,
    Surrendering to your knowing
    I do this for my sake
    Guide me to a place
    Where home it shall make!

Gain time – seeking Ishtar

    By the power of Ishtar
    I (name) now seek
    Stop time to only a heartbeat
    Minute by minute and nothing has passed
    For time stands still
    Until I complete my task!

Gossip – betrayal of trust

    Violation was my soul with you
    I give you a gift of pain too.
    Vengeance is not what I ask
    Just that you suffer
    For putting on that mask.
    It be sent,
    Not returned
    I blow a kiss!
    Let the spell be sent
    No more bliss
    For the pain you meant!

Honesty

Friend or foe,
Let his/her true colours show
Truth or lies,
He/she will no longer disguise
By the Maiden side of three
Show this to me,
Reveal what thou hidest from me!

House of judges – ritual for justice

I call upon the ministry of angels, all spirits of light!
To form a cone of power
Sending forth your unconditional love
In this darkened hour.
I summon about thy guardian and guides
That serve me true! Sent forth in light
To stand beside me to empower this rite
I invoke thee! I invoke thee!
Lend me your power,
Send me thy divine light
So I might direct it,
To make (situation) right!

Break here to perform the spell Seeking Ishtar, as time needs to slow down for the next part of the ritual. Then continue and say:

Sent forth ... the light cometh
And clouded thy minds
House of judges
Ye will listen this time!
Forget what you know
And know what is right
Who stands before you,
Is only of pure light.

By the divine light
To you it now consumes
Undo what are (name)'s untruths
Undo his/her untruths! Undo his/her untruths!
In great haste, shall it be
As it wilt, so mote it be!!!

In circles ... I wait

Am I calling forth power
... or sitting with a silent voice?
Can ye Lord and Lady hear my call?
... or is the only sign of light from the street below?
Coincidence or by chance, Lady luck if you prefer
When do I give in and say,
That I already know the answers to such questions?
Open your heart to magik
Feel its awe, let yourself go!
Lead in life "except your truth"
No more circles shall I follow
As I wilt, now can see
My path in front,
So mote it be!

Inspirations

Ink and feather ...
I hold a torch
That I may see, feel, create
With this light, I will make ...
Sister element hear my call
Silent voices I now wake.
Above the sky ...
To thee I implore

Inspiration within me,
Spark and ignite
Oh gracious muse ...
Touch your light
This I thank,
With my gift of sight!

Internal strength

Thine enemies can try to besiege
I never fall upon my knees!
You may show me pain
Your visions of evil
None will harm me, fall to thee
I bound and tame.

The following is to be used as a daily dedication to bring harmony into your hectic lifestyle. What you perceive as a threat or evil sent your way may not always be so. In using this you will gain courage and the will to know.

Karma's house

Night and mist,
All the space in between
Make clear my home, give it to me!
The one I'm meant to own
What is done can't be true
Reconsider the offer I put forward to you!
Hammer and nails
You built, we sawed
Show me my home, give it to me!
The keys unlock my door
What is done can't be true
This house is mine, not meant to stay with you.

Lady luck

Lady luck, shine on me and say
Lady luck, smile at me and praise
Lady luck, bless me to see
Lady luck, Lady luck, Lady luck!
Times it all by three,
That I can! Only be seen
My life, my miracle
As if but a dream.

Letting go of fear

I set aside all my doubts and fears
I set aside my heartaches and tears
For now I set myself free!
From the guilt of thought
From the everlasting torment
For now I set myself free!
To let my spirit fly,
To leave no more lies
For now I set myself free!
Free from impurities,
Free from negativity
For now I am free!
Free to follow my chosen path.
Free to become one with my craft
Now I am free!
Blessed be she who forgives
And sets me free, I am free!
Free, so mote it be.

Losing the end – all-purpose attainment of desire

This is for you
Not them, though is. Era!
Calleth upon
Not for, but plague
'Tis this what has,
Working bee. Calleth!
Financial security, awoke ...
Shall I you, drown in plague?
Through hard work and riches,
I lose the end
To begin what will
That I may create ...
Abundance,
My desires fulfil!

Lost

Where am I going?
Where am I from?
Mistress of the sky
Help me find where I belong.
Maiden, guide me through
Mother, lay my worries to rest
Gentle Crone, part me your way
Mistresses of the sky, unite
Shine me a ray,
That my path it light.
Blessings to thy moon and stars,
Hail oh goddesses three
By their own moon,
Cleanse and enlighten me
Speak not in those words,

Hear in your tongue
For I your child
To my rebirth, it has begun.

Love is blind

To which means does love hold?
To which end does hold on love?
I open these worms
A can, a tale
Lead me to what thou hast
This now I only see the betrayal!
What you say,
That I would never cast
Then the same … that in you,
My trust was meant to last.
Can you see or black in thought?
You can't hide from pain and sin
That our love
Would torment from within
What to do, when hope has gone. Wait?!
Give a second chance
How can I, when the sin …
You, my lover, can't bear to see
See how you played
How you foolishly lost me!
Not to talk,
Shed a tear
I still feel love
That will never disappear
What to do,
I can't tell
Trust in fate,
Now this shall seal your spell!

Love spell

Bring me a lover and in only time shall it be true
They will speak my name with such a sound
Gaze into my eyes like I was the only
Touch me as if I was, embrace me like I never will.
To look upon thee
Shall be a mirror of what is reflected in me and around this
That they indeed will fall in love with
Not to force love's guiding hand
For he/she will only grow from what they know to be true.
That their search ends here
With their soul intact
That love shall find in me,
What makes love truly happy.

In most instances you would call a particular spell before you would dismiss it, but in the next two cases it is the opposite. The first spell, Magik and the bat, is designed to strip an individual's power in order to protect them from potential harm. To call upon their gifts once more, they will be required to summon the energies in the last half of the spell themselves.

Magik and the bat

Dismiss (invocator):
This is what you did ask
I take away the gift, cloaked!
Not to be revealed, blind to see …
Blind is he/she from the true magik,
I cut and tie
I invoke now the bat!
To all mysteries become a lie.
Hide and bleed, mix and stir
Eyes cloud, hard to see

(Name) will twist and turn
By bat of night, true and told
Bound in his/her own disbelief
To his/her sight,
His/her logical mind shall mould!
I can't say this will come to pass for thee (name)
Will he/she fall down and cry?
When he/she can no longer see …
All the ties to true magik in him/her then will die!
Call (recipient):
Took from me,
What didn't go
I wish to see,
To feel, to know!
Bat once more I call out to you …
Symbolise my energy,
Materialise the gift
Return true magik
Unlock that hidden door.
Release and reveal
No more shall the mysteries be hid
I thank you for this
All doubt I thus possess, I now forbid
Thank you, for time in service
Great bat of night
I send you away, dismiss
Returned is my gift of sight.

The second of the two spells can be used more than once, for it relates to everyone. Most of us portray a hidden side to the outside world, a mask which we show as ourselves in order to be safe from harm. The spell called Magik and the mask was created to overcome this illusion that you have come dependent on; if you keep on a mask, your true self can never be fully expressed and that would leave your magikal practices in shallow territory. There are times when you may need the use of a mask, which is why I have included the other half of this spell. Remember that your power is only as strong as your belief in yourself.

Magik and the mask
Dismiss:
This is not as I did before
God and Goddess, hear my call
Take the mask off and the glamour
For these eyes, two shall see
What thee giveth to me
This is not as I did before
Let what is said, be done
Let what is done, be true
In power you shall lend in time of new.
If I shall call upon the chameleon once more
You shall hear my call

Let our powers be
Let our powers three
For as I will it, so mote it be.
Call:
Lord and Lady, hear my call,
Return to the temple
Do what I ask once more
To the chameleon I call upon
Unlock that hidden door,
Let the glamour shine through
With the mask I can't lose
The power of the mask,
To which I command
Shalt I receive, so mote it be!

Mental blocks

On the wings of angels it shall come
Let my mental blocks be freed
Thoughts of inspiration come to me.

Mermaid money

Maiden of the deep Aquarian sea
Create a whirlpool of prosperity
That heads towards me.
Shall it rain from the clouds
End my financial drought
Encircling me with unforeseen wealth.

Light a small green candle with either yellow or green currency placed underneath it (A$50 or A$100). Let the candle burn all the way down while visualising the magik being sent as the smoke rises towards the clouds. Towards the end snuff the flame out; do not blow out the magik!

Message to you

I put a message in a bottle
To sail across the great oceans blue
Send you my thoughts
Give you my heart.
I work a flower,
To souls be mend
A beautiful rose,
A love that can never end.
Tears is none
Heart be whole
With you entering …
My life, my home, my soul.

Place in a tall bottle the message: My soul mate, to you I love. Then seal it shut with either a cork or lid, ensuring the message remains rolled up inside. Stand by the seashore at sunrise with bottle in hand and, as the tide comes in, throw the bottle high over the sea's edge and let the current take it out to the one for whom your love shall grow.

Order to chaos

It is he whom spirit burns, heart bleeds
Suffering, forcing me on my knees
I've endured all that is, all that can be
Hear my plea!
To wake in early light of day
Cast out!
The negativity at play
To this chaos I do lay
To rest it shall be
Emergence
Of absolute pure,
Dispel forever such negativity!

Real love

Mirror reflections, I don't see
Beauty I have embedded in me
It is where the heart rests,
Mirror is what can be untrue
What matters is in a lover's eyes,
The feeling he/she has for the real you!
I don't care for his/her reflection
Just to return
His/her unconditional affection
As I wilt, so mote it be.

Ring me when you're ready

My circle, between
Around and reflect
Between, my circle
Reflect around me!
Been found and lost,
But nothing incomplete
Only as a whole.
I will never forget
The way I feel about you,
For I am lost without that
Confused ... understandably so!
What is then,
But this circle must go
I thank that I got my ...
One day, one moment
With you, with the real me
Thanks to thyself for setting the truth free.
Whatever a path I shall lead
I will be that man/woman,

Nor no other.
Remember me, don't circle this!
Keeping focused not to tell
Just giving myself complete confidence, honesty
To this I not cast! Nor was a spell
Me, in all to bless
Me, not a circle ... between
Truth and lies, for now know, the circle
Can no longer disguise.
I must and you
Be free, be open
No rules, no lore
Be but us and make it so
As I said and shalt not say,
This I not cast!
And you shall see
For as I wilt, so mote it be.

Sadness

Reverse back the clock,
Don't let another tear drop
Remember what brought on that tear,
Make it disappear!

Scales of truth

I want to know,
Where I stand
Give me answers,
That I demand!
No more hiding
From answers, I do seek
To you I command

To your will I defeat!
Unable to lie or even hide
Let the scales of truth reveal
The knowledge
You have buried inside
Like a puppet on a string
Answers you do bring
By darkness of night
Shalt the truth be in my sight.

Scare

Give me the staff
Flames and fury, I cast
The visions of evil you see
Drive you away from me!

Search for love – overcoming loneliness

For the loneliness,
Suffering no more!
I open up my heart,
Unlock that bitter door.
Shalt the seeds of love, be sown!
Sweep the earth
Find thy soulmate
To which my heart is torn.
Sew the two broken hearts
Bleed into another,
Shall never part
This is what I creed,
This love will find me!
As I wilt, so mote it be.
Burn a tall pink candle on the window sill at night so that your

lover can find their way to you. Surrounding it with yellow rose petals will promote happiness in your union.

Seduction

This spell is to be done on a Friday at sunrise or a new moon. Make a circle with red rose petals on the bed with two roses in the centre. Put a combination of rose (love), musk (lust) and jasmine (attraction) into an aromatherapy burner, leaving some of the oil to anoint the two roses (as you would a candle). Once this is all set up and you have lit a few candles in the room to create the right mood, tie the two roses together with a pink or white ribbon, saying:

This is for tears no longer shed
To bring thy lover to my bed!
Bring him/her to me,
By choice of his/hers
In light and love,
Shall nothing else be right!
Henceforth I then creed
By the Goddess of love, so mote it be!

The tactic we employ to seduce one person may not be effective on another. Try playing this angle and see how you go:

Roses prick,
My heart not bleeds.
Send me a lover,
The one that's meant to be.
Circle be cast,
Faeries make it so
Daughter of the three
Maiden, assist in bringing him/her to me!
Candles lit and oils burn
The mood is set, bed is cold
Passion thus create

All these thoughts of me,
No other shall he/she contemplate!
As I will it, so mote it be.

Self image

I defend, I can't go on this way!
This nature in me that I pretend
Weak as I am, cloaked in fear
I tear the bonds, release and disappear!
Dark is your mind,
Through harsh words and actions
Can't you see?
Through sharp objects,
Pain and internal tears
See all that is me disappear!
I reaffirm my belief in me
I can't breathe in your presence
Through the twisted lies and hatred
I hand myself to you
Not like it was!
Now how it will remain true.
Weak as I am, cloaked in fear
I tear the bonds, release and disappear!
Hurt me, tease if you will
I am open now, my wall between
Break and kill
I make, you take: no more shall this occur.
Let me in, I shall breathe
I am me and not a fake
Shine through your lies I shall achieve!
Weak as I was, I now stand confident.
Believe in myself, I shall

Escaped from your evil
Your lies, your hatred, my hell!
So mote it be.

Sleep

Eyelids fall
Breath of air, gasp
Goddess grant me
A restful sleep that will last.
Pale blue candle
By my bed at night
I light for you, blow out
When I sleep tight!

Stress

Move mountains,
Part the sea
My hands shake now
This strength has slipped away from me.
Aradia cometh
Fill me with your presence,
The worthiness
Take ills and mischievous emotions at play
Rid all this,
To my stress go away!

Success

"I call about the faeries!"
"I call about the faeries!"
"I call about the faeries!"
To ride upon the four winds of Raphael
Raining success with each chime of their bell.

For in the darkness of the night,
They ride out of sight.
By the break of day
In the mist, of a new
So shall my success be true!
In the mist, of a new
So shall my success be true!
Oh to thee fiery sphere that rises high.
I rejoice your birth in dark of sky!
I welcome your bright and shinning rays,
And I thank you for my life
On this next upcoming day!
Oh! Shining master of success,
Shine to me tomorrow and bless
My dreams and goals with miraculous power
Upon then, success and triumph I will be showered!
By these forces unite,
By my will and this rite
So mote it be!

Taking control

Maiden, Mother and Crone
I call all three
To take away the indecision
That surrounds me!
Replace my negative attitude
Dispel all my doubts and fears
Taking away my pain
Leaving no more tears!
Maiden, Mother and Crone
Grant me the chance to be free
From all restraints that have bound my will
By sisters three, as I will it, so mote it be!

Torment

Bodies burn, my soul deep
I reach for him/her,
The harp my bladed tool
Addicted to this, my loss, this loneliness!
Of being without his/her love, the heart aches
Of knowing it can never be enough!
Relieve me from my heart
Stop playing the harp
This love is hurting me!
Though I can't see it now
I wish to be freed ...

Tower plead – attainment of desires

This spell helps to obtain your desires when time is of the essence; it can be adapted to a variety of uses and only takes a few moments to perform. Gather a heatproof container, a sheet of paper and a pen and inscribe the following first verse of the spell:

This is what I creed,
By the burning of this!
(Desire) Unforeseen wealth
Cometh to bestow upon me.

With the heatproof container on one side, place the sheet of paper above it. *Pierce the skin and, before the blood rushes to the surface, light the paper in the centre from underneath it and hold until it burns strongly, then drop it into the container. As the paper burns, it will start to cave in and form a sphere; at this point add three drops of blood and with each drop say:

By the rising of the smoke
Three drops of blood,
To your power I evoke!

*The use of blood magik is always optional: each spell I give that involves the use of blood can be performed without blood. It is only there to heighten the spell in order to achieve results sooner then expected.

Once the flames have extinguished take the container outside, hold it high in the air and let the wind take the ash. If the wind is not strong enough, blow the remainder out of the container and then say:

To the wings you glide,
Obtain my desire
No more worries shall I hide!

After you have completed the ritual, place the section where you pierced your skin into the soil and say:

I thank you, Anubis,
For your strength and beseech
The staff, the power!
Force behind the desire I need
Manifest now in this hardened tower.

Travel

Fly above the flame,
Ride upon winds
Sail beneath the sea,
Walk thy earth with me.
To the elements, I implore
Let me get beyond my door
Set me to travel
To my feet, I feel only gravel.

Cast a circle in the sand with candles burning bright and tall, and incense smoke rising to the sky, and dance around until you finish this rite.

Voices – debt collection

Voices ... as they speak
Come to me what is owed
Inside my head,
The guard was lowered.
Weak! As insanity must
Voices strengthen
Whispers speak
Now I have your voice
No more you, shall I seek.
Found and bound
Voice this if you must
What thee owe me, I receive in full
Or shalt thou whose name I not dare speak
Be inflicted with their own voice ...
Thus will self defeat.
By the passing of the tide, silver I give
An offering to thee!
That I may be mistaken
In the loudness of silence.
In this you shall no longer hide
Return what is mine or ...
By this you pay for what you lied!

Yes and no
Pick one yellow and one green leaf and hold them in the palm of you hand. Ask the question that you wish to have answered and then open your hand wide: the leaf that isn't blown away will give the answer you seek. If by chance they both fly away, then ask another question, for that answer cannot be given. If they both remain still in the palm of you hand, then the answer rests with you (a maybe) and no guidance can be given at this point in time. Pick the leaves and immediately place them in your hand. While holding them tightly in your fist, ask your question and say:

Yellow is yes, green is no
Which way will the answer go?

Chapter 11

Empowerment

You may notice that some of the spells in this book seem to lack some ingredient to empower them; if so, then you have a long way to go. Each ritual, chant and spell within these pages does have the necessary tools to achieve the task that it sets. All that is missing is your involvement with that particular task; at times your will alone is empowerment enough! Remember when casting your magik that the drive to obtain the desired outcome must be so strong that you don't visualise the magik at work, but see the goal achieved! Discipline is what will set you aside from the inexperienced; you will not only seek empowerment, you will become a beacon of that power.

Empowerment through self-discipline
- Train the mind to be open to receive
- Believe in your abilities and exceed them
- Perfect your craft and magik talent
- Use meditation daily to increase your awareness
- Consume a larger portion of greens to increase energy
- Maintain a healthy lifestyle between magik and the physical world

When you are unable to raise enough energy to perform a certain spell, or need assistance because what you are attempting to achieve is beyond your capabilities, you can call upon the help of spirit, the God and Goddess. You have seen that with several rituals in this book I have used the aid of an entity to achieve such things as communicating with spirits which, performed alone, could take days or weeks to get results. While working with spirits is feared by some, there is nothing to fear as long as you treat each entity as you would on this plane of existence. As with the living, there are those who would harm and those who are kind in nature in the spirit world. To illustrate this further, if a man was known as a tyrant and overwhelmed with hatred, then in death would his true nature change? The key to working with spirits is to first educate yourself in the art of psychic defence, and then proceed to learn as much as you can about the entity you wish to work with; everything else you need to know will follow.

Empowerment through spirit

- Don't be afraid to make inquiries
  - Will you honour my wishes?
  - What is your name/purpose?
  - Do you come from the light/unconditional love?
  - Are you here for my highest good?
- Don't accept past history as proof of their good nature; always test them with questions like those above until you are completely satisfied.
- Before an invocation is attempted, know which entity you wish to use, the nature of their power and their origin.
- Always invoke them by name and title.
- Ensure that you thank and dismiss them when you are finished.
- Remember you are in control; when it feels that the entity holds more control, terminate the ritual and dismiss the spirit at once. They are to assist, not take over the ritual or you; this only occurs due to lack of inquiry.

Not all your magikal practices have to be serious, although

maintaining a level of seriousness while delving into more colourful techniques of empowerment can achieve the desired result. The most popular methods of empowerment take the form of earth, air, fire and water, which refers to the use of crystals, incense, candles and oils. When practising Wicca, you can see why this form of empowerment is so widely used: it is due to the correspondence they have with the cardinal points. At the back of this book you will find Appendices A to C have detailed lists of colours, candles, oils and crystals including their magikal properties. Their use for empowering spells is fairly easy to master; just follow the guidelines below.

Empowerment through crystals, incense, candles and oils

- Charge your crystals by moonlight before and after their use to cleanse them.
- Holding a crystal in one hand and your atheme in the other will increase the energy being raised.
- Always light the incense/burner oils an hour before a spell, to ensure the aroma fills the room while you perform your magik.
- Incense is used to cleanse and protect the temple or a circle cast within it.
- The size of the candle is determined by the length of the ritual and the purpose the candle plays. Never blow out a candle when complete.
- Anointing the candles before use is important; try using your incense oils to dress the candle instead of plain household oil. The procedure for dressing a candle is to start from the centre of the candle and move up, covering the entire surface with oil, then do the same moving down.

There is no harm in using more than one technique at a time. I suggest you do just that and experiment until you find which method of empowering your spells suits you best. There are so many other wonderful methods of empowerment such as the use of talismans, amulets and seals, not to mention the traditional Wiccan practice of herbalism.

Akashian seal

This is a seal for empowerment and protection. The bearer of this seal will be given the gift of Akasha. Through the art of invocation and the technique of working with stored energies, I give you this link to the untamed power of the light, a seal to carry, wear and use in your magikal rites.

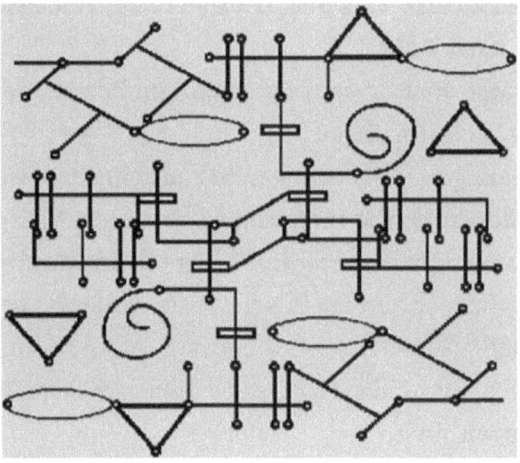

The practical use of the seal is to place it in a locket so that it hangs close to your heart. When using it in a ritual, either burn a candle directly above to invoke its potential or inscribe it on a circular disk and use it as you would a pentacle.

The following practical rituals were designed for the key purpose of raising energy and empowering you by building up hidden energies within, invoking nature spirits and other useful entities.

Burning passion – increase magikal strength

Call:

Eternal I am
Here, stands
Calling about thy fiery friend
I invoke the salamander within
Bringer of light and strength
Giveth me your power
To the salamander I then command.
Make me reign supreme over man.
None is my equal,
Equal are you
Giveth me your gift
Of an invincible source of strength!

Dismiss:

Eternal I am
Here, flies
Burning bright in the night sky
Full of untamed power
Embedded in mine fiery eyes.
Ye salamander I now invoke
Thanks for your gifts,
Now to you I dismiss
Do as I plea, leave only in peace.

Eye of Set – psychic ritual of empowerment

Call:

Beneath thee, are you
Sands cold and of skies red
Oh mighty Set! I command thee to attend
Robed in you, worn is me!
I am power, you are weak!

Bring in your knowledge
I implore
Darkened fury unleash,
Bound thy spirit door.
Cut through your evil,
Restrain the hatred
Steal your strength do I
To release your magik,
Control the power
By will of my third eye.
Dismiss:
Robbed of kindred,
House of smiles
Horus slay the evil in mine own!
Take Set,
Rid and dismiss.
All pains and eyes misused
Like not in day or by my house
Take his power before it's abused.

Mummification rite

I have developed a method of entering an altered state of consciousness that can be used to enhance practices such as astral travel and meditation by adapting the main principle from the Egyptian art of mummification. Not as primitive as performed in ancient Egypt, the aim of this rite is to eliminate all outside sensations that may hinder the altered state of conscious you are trying to achieve. To better describe the dynamics of this technique, I refer to the art of meditation. In the initial stages of meditation, you cannot help being aware of your body and your surroundings, and even when reaching a deeper state of meditation you still run the risk of outside interference. My technique allows you to overcome these obstacles. It gives you the ability to let go of your physical shell and shift awareness from your surroundings to an uninterrupted altered state of consciousness.

The use of sensory deprivation is not new, although its practice in magik is rare. It is simply a process in which you deprive the body of one sensation, which heightens another. Combining this theory with the adopted principle of mummification, "the wrapping of the mummy," deprives you of all external sensations, which only leaves room for internal sensations to grow and be received.

Mummification ritual
- Gather 6 restraints, either ropes, cords or leather belts.
- Collect 1 large white blanket and pillow.
- Perform the ritual at night, skyclad.
- Remember the breathing exercise.
- Cleanse the body, by either taking a bath or using a smudge stick.

- Spread the blanket out on the floor with the restraints near the edge.
- Lie in the middle of the blanket, your head over the edge resting on the pillow.
- Bring in the two sides of the blanket, forming a cocoon around you.
- Now use the restraints to bind you within the blanket, but don't tie your arms inside the blanket at this point.
- Then start tying yourself at the toes, above the ankle, below the knee, on the shin, then the stomach, and finally the waist.
- Now place your arms inside the blanket by your sides (it should be loose enough so that they can be removed).
- You are now ready to enter an altered state of consciousness.

Send forth power

When it comes to working a spell or practicing ceremonial magik, getting the desired result does not come naturally straight away, especially when following a solitary path. This is not to say the outcome will not be achieved but, when casting alone, you only have your own power and ability to fuel the spell, and in some cases you may not have the expertise or ability to raise enough energy for the desired impact. Sending forth power is a technique that involves the building of energy which amplifies your own power far more than you can achieve alone. The method underlying this technique is for raising energy to its highest level, then sending it out to a person in need, for instance, an ill family member or a fellow practitioner who requires more power than they possess. The following meditation can be adapted so that the power raised is given to you, simply by directing the energy built back into yourself instead of another person, which in turn will cause your own energy to surpass what you are otherwise capable of achieving.

Send forth power meditation

Sit in a circle facing the east, element of wind! This is for its importance in the creation and sending of energy. Go into a light meditation, breathing in for six seconds, then holding, then breathing out for six. Breathing always plays a part in meditation, in order for the practitioner to achieve a sense of calm, and a sense of separation from their physical shell. In this meditation breathing is also used to invoke the power of the east and at the same time reaffirm the goal of raising energy.

With each breath in, say:
I invoke the East and raise the winds,
With each breath out, say:
Send forth (recipient) power in this needy hour.

Continuing to breathe at a slow pace, picture your body sitting in the circle from above. Watch this image start to spin as your energy emerges from your heart as a golden light and expands into the circle. Spinning faster and faster, it grows stronger, continuing to spin until finally it shoots up over your head, leaving only what seems to be a pyramid of mass power. At that moment you feel yourself pulled back into your body, as fast as the energy shooting over your head. Now you are back in your body, you feel the power surging through you, at the same time feeling the energy spinning all around, although at a much greater pace. At this point you notice you are no longer there! These feelings have become so intense you are now a beacon of light. Shoot your light, your power, with all your might! You must have an overwhelming desire, a strong drive capable of sending it without delay. As you direct the energy raised, say:

To the east I direct!
To (recipient) whom need it best!

You will feel a pull on your heart as you send forth power. Remember at all times that you are not draining your own energy, but sending an extension of your magikal self. The key is to embrace this sensation, for all the energy is being sent through you. You are a beacon of light, a channel for the power to travel through. When you feel the power has entirely passed through, you will notice a light sensation over your body, a slight tingling vibration. Once you have sent the energy, bring your concentration back to raising your own energy, feeling it build up again. While the circle is still spinning, direct this energy into your heart and the circle will begin to slow, coming to a halt when you have transferred all the energy into your heart. Sit for a moment and concentrate on your breathing; feeling calm and at peace, relax your whole body. It is time to ground yourself, and send off any unwanted energy that may be unstable. Start from the head, working your way right down to the toes, releasing all undesired energy/negativity into the ground. Once finished, you can continue with your magikal practices, but be sure to close the circle when done. Blessed be!

Solomon's key

A battle between light and dark best describes this ritual of words. When you come to a crossroad when you feel you are facing a greatness in your evolutionary quest, you must come to terms with the phrase 'absolute evil' for no such force can exist. No force other than the universal energy can be greater than a being of light and divine power, as you are on this physical plane here and now. Fear is a mindset you can overcome. I have created this ritual in the pursuit of my philosophy: this is the point where you awaken your soul to the true potential of magik and eliminate the illusion of fear that plagues your life. I do not propose to eradicate fear. That in itself would be damaging, for it would allow you to make clear judgement in the face of evil. Where magik is concerned, fear can cause you to reach a point where you are unable to expand your consciousness or, worst-case scenario, result in you losing your faith.

Solomon seems a worthy adversary as a powerful magician who delved into the dark side of magik. His talismans and spells are still used today because they are infused with great power and knowledge of the universe; thus the use of his keys for tapping into the greatness of his magik. Light one black and one gold candle, then say:

Solomon, key, door he cast
Celestial knight within the day
Runic scribe, key be shown
Door to darkness and hidden nights
Key, unlock Solomon's sight
Scribe be none, key, inner space.
Solomon, help me conquer mine enemies
To your evil I can face!
Sorcerer, none equal have I
Power as great, your darkness divide
Key thou surrender,
No magik bounds now have I.

Each person over time develops their own style and ways of empowering their magik. The sole aim of this section is to give you a feel for the different methods of empowerment. Then, when it comes to performing a spell, you can do it with passion and excitement, and at the same time keep in mind the seriousness and determination that will see you achieving your goals.

Unlock secrets – awaken psychic ability

Hail to thee, Thoth, oh ancient one
Keeper of the Akashic records
I implore you,
I command this of you!
Oh mighty Thoth, giveth this to me

Mental and psychic clarity
For you hold thy key
Unlock great power for me!
I cast about this rite
Teach me all your magik
By the darkness of night
Unlock my power
Grant unto me this,
In this magikal hour.
I command this of thee
Speak those sacred words
That will unlock the magik within me!
In this magikal hour
Through space and time
Thoth, make it mine! So mote it be.

Vision quest

A white dagger, this I need
To mend and sow,
Find a path I already know.
Release from questions,
Give up the search
The path shall find me
Open and clear
I see all the signs
I trust, my fear disappears!
Lady, be with me
Not hold thy hand
Vision quest lead me
Here where I stand!

Part IV
The broom closet

Chapter 12

Book of shadows

Creating a book of shadows is a fulfilling and rewarding experience. All you should put into it is whatever you truly believe in and, if you are as passionate about your craft as I am, then writing a book of shadows will come naturally. It is no different from a diary. This is to be your magikal diary, a journal in which you will write all your spiritual experiences and ritual practices. Keeping track of the outcome of your spells and rituals will enable you to look back and see if there are any trends or common failures that could have been the result of poor planning, for instance, you performed a spell on the incorrect day. As with any journal, you should record all your rituals and spells in the book of shadows and keep it up-to-date. Keeping such a book is not as easy as simply writing down all your information, because a book of shadows is a part of your faith and, as you evolve and change, it should reflect that. I have had several different books of shadows and, when each one is completed, it is revised and later translated into another, because as I learn and grow so too do my journals. Each time I perform a ritual or cast a spell, my awareness shifts, taking my book of shadows with me. As you delve deeper into the realms of spirit, you look back at what you have written in the past and see that you now have one more piece to the puzzle of life. You realise that your book of shadows is alive and full of your potential.

A different approach to a book of shadows is what I call a book of secrets. Similar in nature, this type of journal incorporates your entire spiritual experiences and ritual practices into poetic form. I use this technique to help drive out emotions and the experience of what occurred. This is a form of automatic writing, as when you channel an entity to write through you with your hand, but instead of channelling a spirit you channel the hidden power within yourself. To give you a look at my work, I have included some texts from my own book of shadows. Some will hide their true meanings and others will be clear, but they all come from an experience, either my own or a vision for another.

Alive on the dance floor!

Letting go of yourself, the future and fear is the first step towards mastering the power within. This text is an exploration of energy that can be raised simply by letting go and becoming part of the music; a song is just that: a ritual of empowerment.

Can you feel the beat
Hear its rhythm
Feel the heat?
Open your eyes and see
The world beneath your feet
It's the dance floor that's alive
Be the rhythm, hear the song
Feel the beat, feel the burn
Dance all night long!
Bodies move too close
But never touch
Do you see the lust
Burning up the dance floor?
Can you feel the rush?
The world beneath your feet
Be the rhythm, feel the beat

Dance all night long
On the dance floor
Seduced by music
All you want is more!
Sense its power
Feel the heat
let the beat take control
Alive on the dance floor
Let the rhythm steal your soul.
Open up your eyes
The dance floor is alive
Be the rhythm, hear the song
Feel the beat, set the floor to burn
Dancing all night long!
In this house
Titles don't exist
Pure pleasure!
Sexual desire is all one can resist.
The world beneath your feet
Be the rhythm, feel the heat
Explore the passion, dance real tight
Seduced by music, burning up the floor
Feel the beat, set yourself to flight!
Let the beat take control
Feel the music
Above the crowd you now fly
It's on the dance floor where you feel alive.
Open your eyes and see
The world beneath your feet
Open your eyes and see
Alive on the dance floor is where you'll be.
Open your eyes and see

The world beneath your feet
Be the rhythm, hear the song,
Feel the beat, feel the burn
Dance all night long!
Open your eyes and see
The world beneath your feet
Let the beat take control
Be the rhythm, hear the song
Feel the music, feel the burn
Dance all night long!

The awakening

A little dream a while ago was this. What could it be but the alternate choice I didn't, wouldn't, have made? What if it was made again?

A sequence of events
That results in this
A five-year-old dream
To have surfaced
A tale that was told
Visions of the future
What lies ahead
What has come to be
What is now happening to me.
How could that boy
Know what is true?
How come I didn't tell me
Before the events were through?
If I come to see
Walk that street
As if I were in a dream
Would it be like I'm on a stage
Lines I have to speak

Words I already know?
What if I was to change?
Would it play out the same?
Has my life been altered
Guided by some gentle whispers
Controlled by a fate I already knew?
What if?
But it doesn't matter ...

Beating cage

Fear and doubt: are they a way to protect your heart from getting hurt? Or are they an excuse for letting someone go?

I haven't used a spell
To get me the part
Even seen the script
That shows when we would start
I looked for a moment
Through your words and actions
I didn't know I loved
Even to look at you
Until that day ...
The play was through.
Is this what it's like to fall?
I can't breathe in your presence
Can't stop thinking about you at all
I have little control
Which I'm afraid to give up
With you I know
If I fall completely
I won't be able to get up.
I didn't ask for this
When I went on stage

Just like you to know ...
That I wouldn't have it any other way
To be placed here
In my beating cage!

A better way

What is there? Do we truly wish to see the pain we have caused? Or the justice from which their vengeance came?

I look out of my window
It's night
I see the wind that blows
So cold
Hear the birds that cry
Pain
Why does this live
A lie?
Can't it be like
Now or before?
Why can't ...
They stop this hatred
That war?
Don't tell me this
No laughter
I don't want to see
Defeat
Blind man can't fight
Surrender
We're in flood
Give up
Nation in repent
Too late, look at all
This shameful
Blood.

Between emotions
  Where would you draw the line?
  Love
  Lust
  And passion
  Where do the barriers lie?
  A kiss
  A touch
  Or even sex?
  How come it's so complex?
  Does it start with the heart
  Or thy soul?
  Does it end in a kiss
  Or a tear?
  Why do we hold these feelings
  So dear?
  That body
  That smile
  Even their voice
  Which only leaves you to make
  One choice!
  Love
  Lust
  And passion:
  Which one would you choose?

Blessed child

When working with spirits, angels, the divine, there is one experience that cannot be explained in mere words. It is the moment when your belief in them reaches its peak, and they send you a love that cannot be measured, for it is unconditional.

  I hear her words of wisdom

Echo throughout lands
In the whispers of the four winds
Elements of our Mother Earth
The power she holds in her hands.
When I feel the Earth beneath my feet
A gentle breeze through my fingers
The fiery sun on my face
A cleansing sensation
Of the purest water through my veins
I'm aware of the goddess within.
I feel them running through me
As if to call my name
Through me, like I was her own
Blessed child.

Blind love

The utopia of your true love comes true, then awake to the silent reality of that illusion you call happiness. Love not returned, denial-driven obssession with the one who stole your affection.

Your voice
Carries me
Through the night
Stay ...
Hold me in your arms
Let it be
Forever in that
Moment
Freed from illusion
Separate from
The sun, fear of
Precious void
Darkness take me

Travel through
The night
Live in dreams
Sleep
In your arms
Awake
In my nightmare
Reality of
You
Never there
Me unconsciously
Addicted
To your love.

Breathless

We can live our lives oblivious to love, too busy being run into the ground by the corporate world. Love can't wait for us to wake up. Then you are breathless when you cross their path, breathless when love consumes your body, when you look into their eyes, insatiable.

Naked of flesh, heart be not
No air to speak
Breathless, upon my feet
I need to see, to wake love
I need to be needed as, special
Is this I speak of?
There you or in here
Breathless
I fall upon my knees
Are you real?
I love, but am I enough
Whole, were you?
Breathless

Feeling cold and alone
Beneath the tears and sheets of fear
I wait for you, come!
Wait not any more
If that, then yes
Breathless
Be not and it is
Yearn to love.

Broken house

It is inconceivable, the pain of a child, to picture the comfort zone evaded ...

Tear my skin
Drain ...
The blood
Take my heart out
Leave
Me for dead!
Doesn't matter
What?
You see
I will always
Be me.
You can dress me up
Teach?
Lecture about life
I will still remain me
Even to my throat
You bare a knife!
See the pain
A few words can inflict?
Remember ...

I loved you before all this.
I thought I would give anything
For you to care
To have it all back
But how
Could you do this
To your own?
Then I realise
It is you!
Who tore me away
From my home.

Come tomorrow

To take your own life, suicide, is the problem too great? Are you that unreachable by society? Or is it just that you can't face yourself? Look inside, is there truly no solution, no help available? Admitting there is a problem, then seeking help, is the most crucial step you can take.

I never thought it would be like this
That my home, my life, my job

Wouldn't be as simple as a kiss
I pick a blade!
But its friendly touch I cannot bear
The pain I feel must fade and die
This could take my life
Don't you see?
This is the last hurt that could happen to me
I can't get up
From my puddle of tears
If I slash my wrists now
Maybe my torment will disappear
I forget in this moment
The person who shall find me!
When I take my last breath
Who am I
To put them in that place?
When it is me, death I have to face
The only way out seems so clear
That my sorrows
Once dead
I don't have to deal with
Come tomorrow!

The dark side of love

Sensing that you are unable to leave a relationship can be so overwhelming that you become convinced that your affection is returned, that this person means not what they say, is not who they are when intoxicated. In fact, you feel you are somehow deserving of such emotional punishment.

I drown my happiness
In fear of you
Walk alone

Sitting with friends
All alone it is you
My soul I must
Defend!
Tore my life
Broke me down
Building it
Is not as easy as it sounds.
Falcons come
Wings of news
Emotions I have
None?
Fears I must escape
All this because of you
No more I take!
I give cannot
Letting you go
Goodbye, farewell
Realising now
My little world of hell.

Dead birds

Don't understand, or see clearly ... crystal not even close! There is substance in what we do and say. Truth and lies, empty if not truth and will be revealed. Our choices to make alone ...

How do I begin?
What I've already started
How do I know?
When to hop on
If life is moving too fast?
Couldn't I lose my balance?
A leap of faith ...

This is the heart of indecision
Hard to evaluate our choices
Rather than understanding!
Sacrifice my wings
Die! A part of me
Sign, too blind to see. Birds
Along the sky. Sound
Footsteps off the path
Guardian? Of what's ahead
Foresight. That I must wait
Key ... to the path already
Led, by me, him
No wings of flight
Heaven sent! Angels
Darken rooms. Cloaks
This life then. Stop!

Fear of disappearing into the void of death

My belief is simply this: death is not an end or the beginning, it is merely the transition from one plane of existence to another. It is your body that dies, but it is your soul that remains alive forever.

We're born to die
Thus once we embrace death
We can finally live.
For after death
We truly live
Fear not death
Fear life.

Feather chains of bliss

Your unbounded potential may seem full of hope, a world in which you can find happiness. Not only in magik but in games of the heart, you may play it safe; surrounded by bliss, you may look into the mirror and see not. Under your own spell, you become those untruths you told!

I, no longer me
Release
From the ...
Feather chains
Of bliss!
My heart
Feels not, cold?
Must
Beat again,
Hands washed clean
Separate
It can't be me!
Grip, my soul's escape
Indulge
Routine of you
Hurts, mirror deep
Fear
I won't heal
From suffering
Falls ...
Upon my feet!
Voices
River keys
Whispers of you
Control, I release
From the ...
Illusion
What was?
My feather chains
Of bliss!

Infant man

Look inside yourself: are you scared to face you?
You mend a rattle
Shed fear
Don't know what to do
Hope the problem disappears
It be said, not yet true
Falsehood and lies
Will not consume you ...
No! Happiness, yes
Bring out herself!
Bring out her best!
Not enough to put your mind at rest
In the dark you see a child
Broken rattle, two
Don't want this to happen to your child
The pain you knew.

Hidden fear

We hide from ourselves our darkest fears. When confronted by them, we are unable to see the truth. What are we truly afraid of?

I see you there ...
In the shadows
Staring
With daggers in your eyes
Peering out at me
Waiting to escape
The darkness.
I look closer
Deeper into your eyes
Only to see ...
A vision of myself

Hidden in the shadows
Drowned in fear
Waiting to be free.

In the darkness he waits

Is it death we're afraid of, or is it what happens when we die?
Hanging from the mountain top
As it crumbles between my fingers
He creeps up on me
I can feel his breath
On the back of my neck
His determination stirring my fear
All this in a single moment
When hope disappears.
Uncertain of my fate
I think back to before I fell
Knowing that I could have gone back
But instead I continued to climb
I realise now the importance of time.
My hands are slipping
As the gravel falls through my fingertips
I feel him closer now
Placing pressure on my fragile grip.
While sensing tiredness through my joints
The muscles in my arms weaken
Causing one arm to drop to my waist
Unaware of the impact
I lose all control ...
And begin to fall
My body hits the ground at great speed
Leaving me here
For I did not die at all.

Still hanging from the mountain top
The fear has gone
The pain has stopped
There he is, standing bright and tall
He is not the villain, not thought of at all!

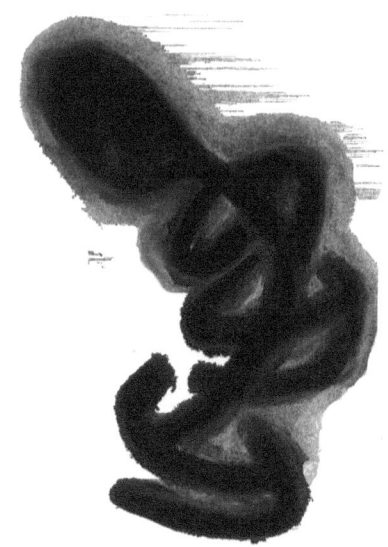

Joyful suffering

Pain in most cases is an indication that something is wrong. Looking at this closely, we may assume pain is indeed a natural response by which our physical body tells us we are still alive.

See the pain
That others have felt
And you'll see you have no pain.
Pain is but a desire
The desire to hold on
Hold on to that one thing
One thing
That won't hold on.

Lost in your eyes

We look for the moment. That moment when time stands still, when all that exists is you and that special someone. To be caught up in their awe, to fall completely in love. Having said that, what if you were the only one to fall?

> When you wake up and look at your side
> It would have already been goodbye
> All the time and the chance
> Didn't know I lost you in the second glance
> In secret you dreamt of touch in sin
> Holding the wrong one you know now wasn't me
> Gave up a moment
> Caught in time ...
> Where you, my dear, were meant to be mine
> I know now how foolish I was
> Falling in a moment and letting go of doubt
> I would do it again!
> To be frozen in time
> Though it won't be you
> This I speak ...
> Does not have a boundary line.

Love is this

No one can tell you you're in love. There is no way to measure it, nor is there any way to predict when and with whom it will occur. All you can do is embrace this feeling, for that is all it is; or is it?

> I live in moments
> Built on time
> You enter my world
> Don't you see?
> Time has altered
> All I can feel is ...

You and me!
I look at you
Just once
A day goes by
You touch my hand
And time slips from me
A kiss, an embrace
In that moment
My heart begins to race.
I look around
At my world before
Realising now
You are all I live for
Don't you see?
Time has altered
We stand still
I come up to breathe
To see days gone by
In only a second
That moment
You looked into my eyes.

... a leap of faith into the fires of hell, so warm, a bitter sweat. She does not feel the pain and agony, for she is in love. The spears are like roses and the chains that bind her dying soul feel like her lover's embrace. Love can be blind, numb from the truth ...

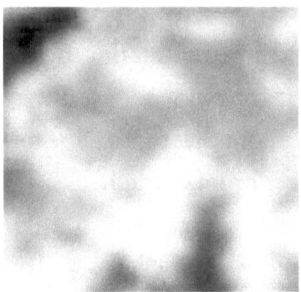

Me

No interpretation can explain the complexity of this: a stare through space and time, that is all I will say.

Let the hour be struck
Whispers travel afar
Blind sight and emotions freed
Images of you come to me.
Angel death and lost thoughts
Unravel restraints!
And reveal desire
Hopes and dreams hasten within
The hour.
Visions be seen, will be seen
By ninth of nine I seal this Clock
By ninth is him, Clock
Hour be done
This spell then stop!

Mysterious as she

Faith when strong can move mountains. Belief in that divine nature which structures your faith is where you draw strength from. You must know without a doubt that this divine force exists and no proof is needed; your belief is proof enough.

I awake in the morning
To the sun's gentle rays
Cold winter winds brush my cheek
As she passes my way.
Lighting a candle in my temple
Flames rise high
Smoke from the burner
Are smelt across the morning sky.
I go about my daily routine

Run a bath? But instead a shower
For I must get ready
Within an hour.
Water falling on my naked skin
Purifying my body and washing away the night
While getting myself ready for work
She seems out of sight.
I hear the sounds of birds in the tree
And I know she is all around
Sure as the water trickles over me
That she can be found.
Not only in magik is she present
But in the morning rush
And throughout the day
She doesn't need enchantment
Nor potions and spells
She is always there by my side
In the candle flame
Or the gentle wind that blows
Even in a stranger's eye
You never know.

New battle, old fears

It is common to have a fear of dying, but when that fear begins to monopolise your life then it's time to let go. Live life in the present moment, instead of the uncertain future.

It's time
To face
Face thy fears
Of dying
For he has come
To take me

Away from here
Away from the pain
Pain caused by my addiction
To survival.
Though I know it's time
I'll continue the fight
To live without fear
Of dying
Living as if there's no fear
Fear
For that word ...
Brings pain itself.
I wish to live
Live now
Not before
Not after
Just now!

The power of solitude

We dwell in our own silent company and society proclaims that we are alone. We choose to move without the presence of friends and members of that society call us sad ... as if happiness can only be derived from the company of others. Then who is truly alone: society or you?

Sitting, staring at
Pale blue walls
Thinking of chimney sweeps
And butterflies
Why?
Bored, gazing at
Clouds forming
Rainbows dissolving
Sadness

As tears run down
Crying out
Silence
Loneliness
Broken friendships
Dying heart
Being apart
From society
Life?
You, staring
Curious
Never talking
Always pointing
Alone!

Routine

Try to put a label on them, put yourself in that box. Is there room or do you need another? The chaos theory ... maybe not, just life.

Schedules and rosters
Work
Pagers and mobile phones
Connectivity
Organise and prioritise
Lists
People and places
Social
Family and friends
Annual
Does this box suit you?
Try another
Still not a perfect fit
Start all over!

No time, a watch
That's right!
At work, no mobiles
Will need to organise
A list!
People to call regarding this
Weekend's ...
Social event
We are
In effect, our
Routine.

Secret love

Written for Kylie: may you find every bit of happiness that comes your way. I send you my love and celebrate your life each minute of every day!

I stare at you for hours at a time
And nothing
I look back at how you've made me feel
From the first time we crossed paths
From the first time you spoke to me at last!
I felt love, the love that's carried me this far
Nowhere
No closer to you
Or anything else.
Still I stare
Stare at that smile I love so much
So sweet, so pure
Stare at your boyish looks
So cute, so irresistible
Still I stare uncontrollably at you
Stare and stare and stare!

I stare at you from so close
But yet far away
Until that day you turned around
Looked straight into my gaze
I had no time, knew I couldn't stay.
All I could do was hide my face
For when you caught me
I felt scared, shy
Tears ran from my eyes.
Then you smiled ...
Surprising me, as if you knew all along
The love I felt for you
You had for me
Taking that one chance on love
Is what now makes me so happy!

Shattered dreams and lonely knights

When you find that special someone you believe is 'the one,' love them with all your heart and soul. Looking into their eyes and seeing only emptiness, a side to them you wish wasn't there, knowing your love will never be returned: in this moment the fairytale romance never existed!

I lay my head on my pillow at night
Longing for your touch
For you to enter my world again
Bringing back the love I miss so much.
I try to be strong, not to cry
Though tears stream down
From painful memories of us in love
Which I can no longer hide
This is why I feel it's all a lie!
I know it's over
But it can't be true

Think about all we've done
I am still in love with you.
Thoughts racing as tears fall
Lying awake
Now in a pool of tears
Realising you've opened up
My darkest fears.
Trying so hard to come to terms
With decisions made
Unable to decide
If it was me who was played!
I cry out in desperation
Unsure of what I feel
All I know is my love for you
Is all that's real.

A single moment

Is this my life? We don't want to see that the one we have come to love is someone else. An unpredictable moment will appear when we have no choice but to see such an unimaginable reality: being alone!

When I'm lying here
Here in your arms
I don't feel your heartbeat
Mine slowly drifting away
What is it you've done
That makes me no longer want to stay?
I woke up
Hoping not to be in this place
Why?
Now! You show me your true face.
I loved you
Well, at least I thought

When did I sign up
For your cruel games
Is it me who is to blame?
I am stronger than before
From these trials I have fought
Who are you now
To keep me in this place?
It is time to leave, now!
At least I never lied to your face
Nor showed you an emotion untrue
I hope that one day ...
You can know love the way I do.

Strip

Inspired by your body touching mine, sensual love free from guilt, forbidden passion explored outdoors in secret.

Look
At how we are
Touch
My body
Warm
One perfect being
Taste ...
The soul of our love
We are one of a kind
Naked?
In the eyes of my lover
Beautiful
In the eyes of my man
Stripped free
You
Of me

Sensual sex
Bound!
In ropes and chains
Stand naked
Not me ...

Thoughts of you

Setting up walls so you cannot be hurt by the ills of society may seem to protect you from suffering. But if this wall shields you from the one thing you yearn for most, a love that will never end, will you take the chance and break down that wall?

This is what I see
Of me ...
Darkened escapes
Shadows
Illuminating fear
All derived from?
I sit
Thoughts racing
Unaware
Damage caused
Time
Stands still now
Blind
To the cause
Reluctant
To feel
Let you in.
Fear
I might be hurt
The truth be known
You care

For me ...
Why is it hard
To breathe?
Could I be
Loved?
I hide from its truth
Age gone by
By now is love
I stand a chance
Of losing all the above.

Transmogrification

Channel in the truth and stand face to face with who you will be.
It was as if a light bulb came on
And I finally understood
I pulled my life like a puppet on a string
Let go, they said, so happiness we can bring.
What are you casting for
When all around you is magik?
What spell would you use
When the end is unclear?
Close your eyes and let go
Mirror what is true!
Release from the magik, not to bind or lose your place
Finding yourself here!
Standing face to face.

Twins

Separation anxiety: try to break us down, separate a greater understanding.

    Can you see me when you're not here?
    I close my eyes as if you've never left
    Can you find me when my home you don't know?
    I can feel you 'here' wherever you may go
    Can you hear my thoughts of you?
    My breath on your name?
    Is this just a fading tale of two?
    Will I wake from this lie?
    Or is this a dream come true?
    Do you inside feel me
    When I'm not there?
    My heart slips a beat
    As if I'd die just to be with you
    Do you think of me
    When in space you sit and stare?
    My love ... I wish I could tell you this story
    If it be fate, to who you are lost

Then he shall find!
Am I loved? Do I still love?
Will I wake? Or is this a dream?
Twins, one of a kind
Separated by a force unseen
What would it be like
To find your other half?
Would you let it slip, fall apart?
Don't know what you've got
Until you feel this ...
A broken heart.

Chapter 13

Psychic art gallery

Next is what I call the psychic art gallery, a collection of artwork that has been channelled through me by spirit, both foreign and familiar entities. I will not interpret them, but leave that up to you. What I will do is tell you a little about the nature of the images. The two figures that appear first, of a man and a woman, are my closest guides. The rough image that follows was sighted above a bed. The next three consist of an entity I invoked from a property, and the last of the seven is the voice of spirit teaching me one of the many gifts I now possess.

Before attempting to channel an entity, you must first understand what you want to achieve in making contact with a foreign force; realisation of your mental limitations and understanding of those hidden forces should be explored before any further progress. Identifying those souls you wish to commune with is the next step. It may seem easy at first, but remember that any entity can access the Akashic records, meaning they can relay your entire life to you as pseudo-evidence of their authenticity. Never assume one way or the other. Be sure to ask questions until you are certain that they are what they claim to be. You are putting your trust in them to guide you, send a message or show you a vision of a desired outcome. You must not give yourself over lightly, or at all! Whatever the case, they cannot lie about their name and their true purpose.

I will give you an example. If you were to ask an entity if their name was Alexander, then their answer could be "yes." Then, once you had supplied them with the basic information, all they would need to do was search Akasha to prove to you that they were indeed this person. I myself have fallen victim to an entity by trusting what they have shown themselves to be. Remember, if there is any room for doubt, then dismiss them from your temple immediately. A true source of light will understand your requests and will not need to convince you either way, nor be offended by your sudden request for them to leave.

Although I drew the images throughout, I do not claim to be an artist. This gallery is merely the extension of spirits' message to me through artistic expression. I am a channel who receives inspiration from spirit, and my impressions are visions of their truths. The illustrations are not interpreted by me; I leave that up to you. They all convey an important message, whether great or small. However, I have provided a closer look into two particular pieces, due to the relevance of their messages. The first is "Rite of passage," which then goes into more detail when it becomes "Spores of light." The same principle applies to "Reborn into death," which in turn flows into "Mirrored souls."

Red feather

Lady of sands

Silent voice

Rite of passage

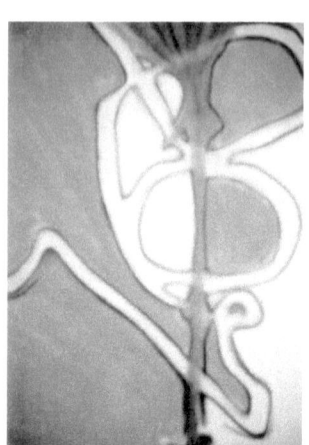

Spores of light

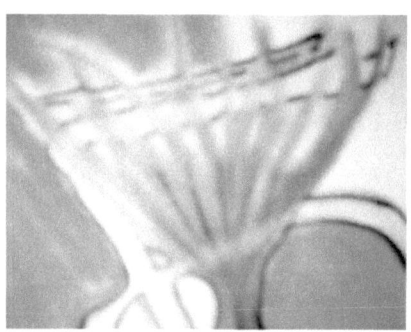

Reborn into death

Mirrored souls

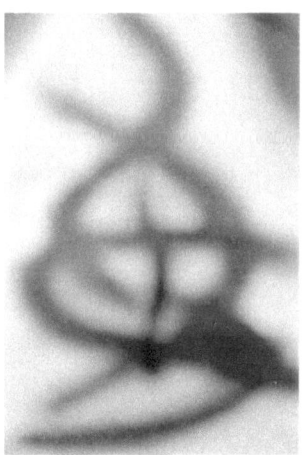

Escape freedom

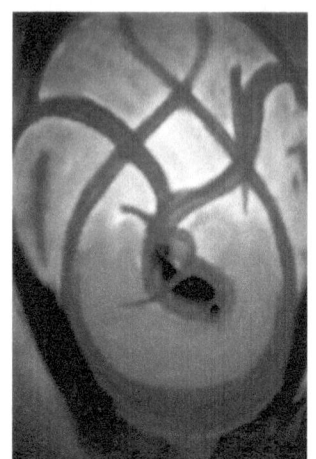

Painted man

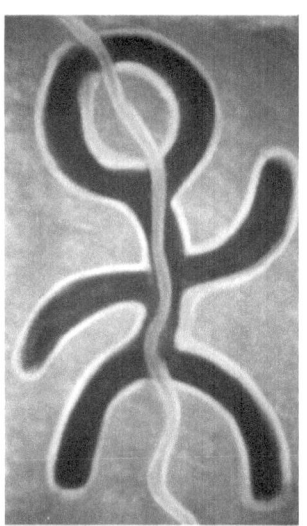

Part V

Final notes

Awakening or psychosis?

> *Grant me the serenity to accept the things I cannot change, the courage to change the things I can, and the wisdom to know the difference.*
> The serenity prayer

During extreme states our underlying personality, the identity with self that we hide from the world, begins to surface. This results in what Buddhism describes as suffering, distress, as the overwhelming influx of spirit awakens our perception. These usually subconscious traits, sometimes referred to as the "shadow," are a clear sign of spiritual emergence. The distinction between this and psychosis lies in knowing how to get back up after the fall (of the ego); difficulty coping, withdrawal from the present, resistance and inability, and fear of change are all characteristics of clinical psychosis.

I would like to say my awakening was without incident, that I came to the realisation of my truth, let go of my limitations and bravely accepted the integration of spirit, but that wasn't the case. To the world I was known as Nathan, while in secret I had adopted the name Ethean (see Magikal names in chapter 3) to become one with magik. Unaware of the impact this had, of the fires burning within, I slipped into darkness, and when I awoke there was no shadow as I stood in my truth, that I am magik ...

From the darkness

To illustrate the power of magik, I will share my story ... it may be more for you! It takes place on many levels of existence and, if you delve a little deeper, you'll see my struggle through many levels of consciousness.

"Practise as if it be your last breath, and the first! An obsessive love affair"

This is my life and I have surrendered to it. Some say they practise magik, but how long do you need to practise for? I myself am magik: if you ask me, I'm only human; if you ask Ethean, then pull up a chair. He is my every breath, my last and the first I ever took alone. Not me, my ego. Look inside and see Ethean: beyond my eyes are his. There inside me, what you see is the darkness you feel, the absence of reality, when voices call out! He is my truth, my unconditional love, my soul divine incarnate. Back to my story; sorry for that, he tends to focus out and finish what I've started, leading me where I need to go. See what I'm saying? But I haven't said it yet! Already at the end without even beginning, see how human we can be? Deep end I'll start and deep end I'll stay.

I had a killer addiction! A habit, a cycle. If there was a bottom I would have crashed through, I was so far from a sense of reality from four years of drug abuse. You think I'm all powerful, that magik comes easy? Think again. Work it! Own it! Live it! Be it! Magik is living and breathing all around you. Take your last breath, I dare you, and surrender to the magik. Don't fool yourself that I am suggesting drugs are a way to magik; myself and many others risked losing everything for drugs. Falling victim to drugs and my denial almost led me to losing both my best friend and my own life. Also my truth, the magik, my purpose for living, which you know is to share the magik with you!

Little moments helped me to see. A little faith kept me alive. If you're a survivor of such a ride, then you'll know how dead you were inside, removed from consciousness, from yourself, from the drug, from any sense of reason, only where the next fix would come from.

I looked at myself and saw what everyone else was doing wrong. So I left those crazy people behind to protect my sanity. Here is something taken from the book of secrets but now time to share, to gain a better understanding of the disillusions of happiness, pain, my story:

Untitled, unsure, unimaginably unlike me ... behind paradise

The inside out. From the dance floor to the bathroom tiles. Chasing the ultimate high: temporary, thus unreachable. Always chasing, always high. Is this addiction or is paradise a lie?

If I danced with the devil to see if I could, surely then! She knew I would stay.

I was led to believe I'd found heaven, thought I felt it. Time stretched ... there were weeks in a day, months in a week, years of memories too vague to recall. What was heaven? What I saw in others, perfection! A little of my journey seemed lengthy. This is life, I was told. Those who disagreed seemed to vanish. A new journey would unfold.

"How many people does she have to hurt, how many names does she have for me to play? Until I stop going back to her, making this addiction ok!"

That gave me strength, just to walk away. If I slipped, I was so scared. There she was, right beside me, on another honeymoon. I didn't even know she'd got me there. Until it was too late, but I didn't know ... remember, I'm in heaven, this is life! Just ask me to stop and I'll see that you go.

Can you follow this? Try and reason using that logic for four years and see how many jobs you go through, how many times you move, how many circles of people you meet. I didn't say friends! You become too paranoid to have friends, all you have is your vicious circles of drug-induced truths and lies. You build foundations to hide the fact that there is a problem, a habit, a situation you are unwilling to face. Reality seems clear: it says the drug is providing you with all the comforts of home, so you won't realise the drug has made you lose your home and the discomfort is in fact the drug-inflicted psychosis. Try putting your life and faith into a book, take off the mask and wear your scars. Following a path of light, whether it be spiritual or through magik, the truth is all you need. Going through your heart is all you need to remember; the rest is up to the divine presence in our lives. Sometimes we just need to allow ourselves to believe and ask for guidance ... a ray of hope!

Truth and lies

Lies are what we tell ourselves in the beginning, for they are the truth we are facing. Yes, it all starts that way and, yes, it is the time of your life, be honest! All you know is how it began; once you're there, you reinforce to yourself that's the way it has always been, unaware of the addiction you have adopted to change all that you knew as your truths.

Lies: it's recreational, just on the weekend with friends, only once in a while, it keeps you going, keeps you awake, alert.

Truth: just on the weekend? You go out Thursday and Friday, sometimes Saturday. We'll drop a few and find ourselves in another day. Then a recovery session! It doesn't matter what day, there'll be a sesh waiting to happen, someone begging to be the wannabe DJ. Sunday session, time to chill out. Sound good? Let's drop again! One more, and what about work on Monday? Go back a second: we dropped a few on Thursday and another to kick start the party, now it's Sunday and we'll drop more so we can relax. Practically Thursday again and the night is young; actually it's during the day and we're at recovery! This is called the rollercoaster: once you're on this you won't have to worry about work on Monday. You've lost your job for being absent ... don't tell me you went to work! Imagine the state you were in, the state you think is solid gold!

Lies: it's a cheaper alternative to alcohol, $35 a pop and off you go, take two and there's your night and a little more!

Truth: $50 and they don't know me, $35 is standard, $22 and you're in deep, $17 and just forget it, you're drowning in something I cannot share. See where I'm going with this? The cheaper the habit, the deeper you fall: you take one to kick off and two to keep going; four years later it's one in your morning coffee and five to kickstart your night, then it goes for three days. You've been known to have fifteen in a single night. Three and most would overdose, but we're talking about addiction, not recreation. Having no real control or choice, only the subconscious need to abuse yourself in order to wake up in this techno-church where you keep yourself in little worlds of hell. Ask me while I was there and I'd have replied, "I'm having the time of my life!"

You're not getting it, it's called drug abuse, addiction. The start I'm sure you can figure out is colourful and nice. Try having a more affordable Saturday night, but that's not me. I have control, I don't need drugs, I can stop any time. Oh yes! I see you every Saturday night, it's starting! What to take next, where will the next high come from? It's never ending, always starting. That's the bottom line when talking about the cycle of addiction, chasing that ultimate high. Each time it's closer, but each time you get further away, deeper into addiction and use of other drugs, all in search of this high you speak of but never will find. Let's face it: at that stage, I was no longer there.

Breaking through

It was a day spent on the beach, blue skies and all. Why not drop one and go for a swim? Sound like fun! Drugs distort reality, so we had no idea of the changes in the surf. I swam back to shore with my friend still out to sea. Then I noticed that she was being dragged towards the rocky cliff face by a strong current, and it sparked something inside me: "You have the choice of whether she lives or dies." I dismissed it immediately: "I can't choose, I'm not God!" Under she went. I was still unsure that it wasn't all in my head, watching as she drowned, not resurfacing. Then again, that feeling, and I knew. With no time I went in and swam underneath her, raising her and cutting myself on the rocks. It's strange how, at a moment like this, we don't question how we can save this person, where we can find the strength and breath; we just risk our lives, knowing that it's right. Don't think that woke me up, because I was "in control" of my habit, I wasn't an addict!

A year or two later (who can tell on these journeys?) my friend came back. Both of us had work troubles, but try and tell us that. With my newfound wisdom of admitting to my addiction, it was time to "road trip" out, which just gave me an excuse to blame on my self-circumstance. CRASH! I woke up in a cold sweat, as uncontrollable tears streamed down. At one of our stops we chose to make camp and spend the night. In the early hours it began, and not until after the fact did the warnings stop. After I woke, I was overwhelmed with the sense that I had not been written in the story to come, that my life would be reset in the morning drive ahead. What could I do? Spend my life at the campsite, or follow the signs and let my faith be my judge? CRASH! I remember, even before the event the car windows were fogged up, sending a chill between us two. Just as they cleared, we knew it was too late. All I can recall is how everything freeze-framed as I saw the kangaroo in front of me, I said "I'm sorry" to my friend, I saw a truck approaching, and the car drifted onto the side of the road, as if in a dream sequence.

All I can say is thank you to those involved: without them I'd be a statistic. Wow! But I still didn't believe we had been put into such a dangerous situation. It was a killer addiction and time didn't exist. I ended up in shock, in a new place ... no car, no money, no job, just a killer addiction and a credit card or two! It all just seemed to go up in smoke, that is, I smoked it all away. Let's go back to the beginning, remembering circles, remembering your connections.

"Live as you are and let it shine through your every day. Child, I have this to pass on: that I love each and every one of you. We never judged you for these trials and pains, for this was your test to fail; passing in another way brought you closer to your truth. Ethean, be reborn into what is."

The message was received as I'm typing these words. This is the life of a channel: having someone else always butting in. I'm sure they'll kick me for that remark! So here I was, heavily under the control of a destructive drug, and in the midst of it all he spoke: "*It's over, I can't do this ...*" Silence filled the room; at this stage my partner and I had people around, remembering we were at recovery of course! A brief second went by and it came again, but this time the message was clear:

"*I need you to leave. I don't blame you for what is happing to Nathan, but leaving him here won't help. It's over and I'm taking control. I'm here to clean up the mess. Nathan has surrendered, knowing that I would have protected him. Sorry, but you must leave! I will not leave him like this, leave while you're still here.*"

Not everyone's tale is as painful and dark, and not everyone can come out once they're in deep. These are my truths, and through the shadows you can see the embers of light trickle through. I gracefully share my struggles along this journey in a world that now urges me to shed light on circumstances we still prefer to sweep under the rug. You see, what surprised me was not the awakening, but the discovery of a spell I had never seen, written only a few weeks before while I was still unconscious:

Would you hear me if I never spoke,
Lived in a mask and walked with a silent voice?
Help! I, you cannot find.
Alone; then this sadness is mine.
Wake me up from this nightmare.
I let go and fall, surrender and release
Wings all around me so I may soar,
Lift me up above this, if only for a second.
Then I shall know my pain,
Feel it so this nightmare is never dreamt again!

What enabled me to walk away was that my devotion to magik was greater in the end. It was as if I took my last breath and then my first once more. Remember: it's easier to destroy the light within than the darkness all around. Blessed be.

Afterword

Like a contract agreed upon by you and carried out by what's within, that's the butterfly effect. Magik doesn't know what you're trying to say! It knows only to manipulate the world around you based on the key principles within the hidden words you speak. The rules and guidelines, responsibilities and duties, the boundaries which are stipulated in the spell ... Some call it a ritual, others a spell, I know it as a contract. Like any contract, be sure you read the fine print: know what you're casting for! You can't say, "I didn't sign up for this", then re-read verse two, line two. Couldn't you feel the synchronicity? I think you have and didn't know it ... too late now, you've signed up for this journey. Enjoy!

I but humble Hehau
Do seek thy Lord
Arise to me
Amun, my god!
I, Hery Seshta, commander of these
Would you forget my Ka forever?
Lord of the thrones of the two lands.
How long will you hide my face from thine truth of Khu?
Amun! Lord of what is concealed
Reveal what is already led
I, a Rekhet, bestow upon by thee.
How long shall I take counsel in my Ba?
Having sorrow in my Ab
Consider and hear me, Lord Amun!
My god, enlighten my eyes.

Amun grant Sa on thee as slept the sleep of N
Bodies in light, Amun oversee'th.
To enter the land of the west
Step out, N of light!
To besiege Amun in darkness
My Khaibit, as one true Khabs.
Lest thy enemy say: "I have prevailed against him"
Lest those who trouble me rejoice when I step forth, the Ren, I am moved!
But I, Ren (not self), have trusted in your mercy
My Ab shall rejoice in safe passage to salvation of my Khat.
I sing to Amun, to thee
Because he hast dealt bountifully
As I wilt, so mote it be.

Name: _____

Signature: _____

Why are you hesitant? The glossary can't save you this time. With everything you cast, make sure the intent is clear, the means to your end is spell-t out correctly, and the spell contains the appropriate measures to carry out your requests; otherwise it only achieves some outcome, whatever the cost. You responsibility and duty of care as a light worker are to the greater good, the collective consciousness, the oneness of God. Yes, inspirations from this particular contract can be found in Psalm 13, but don't let that fool you: does its intent match your own?

Still wanting more? Find out what else Unfolding Magik can offer you?

FOLLOW US: https://www.facebook.com/EtheanSouleRainbowMedium/
https://www.facebook.com/UnfoldingMagik/

Appendices

Appendix A

Magikal numbers

Listed here are the individual characteristics of the numbers one to nine and how they correspond to you on a personal level. You may be surprised at how accurate they are in describing your true nature.

- **one** — strong will, leader, beginnings, action, independence, ambition, focus, dominance, impulsiveness
- **two** — kindness, balance, partnership, communication, peace maker, empathy, understanding, analyticalness
- **three** — intuition, creativity, expression, sociability, optimism, visionary, enthusiasm, charm, positivity
- **four** — stability, practicality, manager, grounding, loyalty, determination, constructiveness, planner, responsibility
- **five** — adaptability, adventurousness, chaos, unpredictability, freedom, passion, motivation, change, curiosity
- **six** — nurture, harmony, sincerity, diplomacy, love, healing, family, compassion, domesticity, sympathy
- **seven** — spirituality, dreamer, imagination, mental understanding, magic, investigator, philosopher
- **eight** — strength, success, power, cycles, organisation, control, decision making, courage, intensity
- **nine** — attainment, inner wisdom, teacher, metaphysical understanding, inspiration, idealism, selflessness

Appendix B

Colours
for candles, cords etc.

white — can be used in the absence of colour (neutral); cleansing & purification, serenity & peace, healing, protection, faith

green — abundance, prosperity & money, connect with nature spirits, healing, luck, fertility, success & employment

yellow — creativity, communication, mental clarity & visions, happiness, courage, study

blue — superior healing, cleansing & purification, truth, sleep, travel, wisdom, harmony & peace

pink — friendship, romance & love, happiness, divine love

red — passion & sexual energy, fertility, love & lust, strength, power, vengeance

orange — legal matters, positive thinking, success & employment, regain energy, inspiration, authority

brown — healing animals, connect to earth, protect home

black — banishment & binding, conflict, increase power, negativity, divination

purple — success, knowledge, psychic ability, inner sight power, divine light

silver — psychic ability, channelling, stability, advanced power, removes negativity/ evil

gold — luck, success, wealth, protection, justice inspiration

Appendix C

Crystals

agate	courage, change, truth, grounding, health
amethyst	enhances healing, inspiration, purity, protection, divine light
azurite	strong healer, intuition & visions, creativity, psychic ability, power
blood stone	strength, emotional stability, stress, confusion, internal healing, femininity
citrine	cleansing, self-esteem, hope, happiness, regain energy, positive thinking
clear quartz	balance, negativity, amplifies energy, communication, peace & calm, psychic ability
jade	fertility, cleansing, love, wisdom, justice, prosperity, money
lapis lazuli	anxiety, speech, psychic strength, mental clarity, power
malachite	insomnia & sleep, tension, uncertainty
rose quartz	love, fear, negativity, forgiveness, doubt, courage, abundance
smoky quartz	depression, dispel evil, visions, grounding
tiger eye	intuition & insight, strength, centring, power, manliness

Appendix D

Aromatherapy oils

courage musk, bergamot, cinnamon, carnation, rosemary

harmony cumin, rose, basil, lilac, lavender, gardenia, lemongrass, palmarosa, chamomile

healing marjoram, lavender, eucalyptus, myrrh, rosemary, violet, carnation, allspice, jasmine, tea tree, chamomile

love jasmine, lavender, rose, gardenia, sweet pea, clove

luck rosemary, cinnamon, cypress

lust musk, clove, basil, cinnamon, ylang ylang

prosperity (money) bergamot, cinnamon, mint, nutmeg, honeysuckle, almond, cedarwood

protection frankincense, sandalwood, basil, myrrh, cypress, rosemary, rose geranium, cedarwood

psychic ability lilac, sandalwood, rosemary, frankincense, lemongrass

purification frankincense, clove, jasmine, lavender, myrrh, rosemary, sandalwood

sleep lavender

Appendix E

Spell register

Here is a list of all the spells within this book. I have supplied you with this register so you can make note of a particular spell's page-number location and any references to that spell which will enable your rituals to run more smoothly.

Aradia's potion

Anomaly

Auric vampire

Banishment of evil

Bast storm

Best friend

Bewitchment

Blessing evil

Bright star

Burning heart

Burning passion

Candle flame

Celestial pyramid

Change

Cleansing jewellery

Confrontation

Consecration of evil

Contact me

Cooling off spell

Cradled discs

Cradle me

Crone of wisdom

Dare to be happy

Daily dedication

Dead energy

Divine rays

Dragon mist

Enough rope

Escaping fear

Eye of Set

Familiar

Family feud

Foundation

Forgiveness

Frozen fear

Full moon rite

Gain time

Gossip

Healing waterfalls

Honesty

House of judges

In circles ... I wait

Injured butterfly

Inspirations

Internal strength

In threes

Karma's house

Lady luck

Letting go of fear

Lighthouse

Losing the end

Lost

Love is blind

Love spell

Magik and the bat

Magik and the mask

Magik shield

Magikal gate

Mental blocks

Mental walls

Mermaid money

Message to you

New moon rite

Order to chaos

Padded wall

Painful tears

Protection jar ritual

Real love

Restrain anger

Ring me when you're ready

Sacred space ritual

Sadness

Scales of truth

Scare

Scrying

Search for love

Seduction spell

Self-destructive behaviour

Self image

Self initiation

Send forth power

Shaft of light

Sleep

Solomon's key

Soul deep

Spiritual attunement

Stress

Success

Sunny day

Taking control

Tool consecration

Torment

Tower plead

Traffic lights

Travel

Unlock secrets

Vision quest

Voices

Walk alone

Weak threat

Yellow rose

Yes and no

Occult Glossary

Akasha: The ultimate force behind the universe. Compare with Ether.

Akashic records: Every decision, thought and action you perform in life is documented and stored within a vast library, Akasha, which becomes a complete record of your life.

Ankh: An Egyptian symbol meaning life.

Anubis: The Egyptian jackal-god who has the body of a man with a head of a jackal. He is the "guard dog" protector spirit, and the guardian of the astral plane. He is known to stand by Osiris.

Astral plane: The spirit world, the afterlife; where the angels reside and where you go when you sleep at night. At rest, it's as easy as picturing yourself looking back at you; when your perception changes, look around the room and leave your body there to rest.

Astral travel: The process of voluntarily leaving your physical shell in an astral form. It is as an out-of-body experience or projection, the separation of your consciousness from the physical self. You project your self-image/astral form out of your physical shell.

Athame: A knife with a double-edged blade that is used to direct/raise power during Wiccan rituals.

Aura: The psychic body, an energy field that surrounds every living person. It can demonstrate many aspects of an individual, including their mental and physical health.

Automatic writing: The process of becoming a channel through which other entities may communicate with the use of a pen and paper. The entity takes control of your hand and begins to write. A related technique is psychic art where, instead of communication through written words, the entity is instructed to paint or draw a picture of the message. Compare with Channelling.

Ba: Meaning "soul" in Egyptian.

Bast: The Egyptian cat-goddess of fertility and healing. She is the twin of Horus, which is why they have similar properties, although she foresees in the areas of intuition, marriage and the animal kingdom. Compare with Horus.

Bewitched: To have a spell put on you, some negativity or evil that has been sent your way. This can be in the form of magik or by human desires and thoughts.

Blood magik: An old style of magik that involves the use of your vital "life force" to raise magik that enables you to exceed your own energy.

Channelling: The art of entering an altered state and allowing your body to be used as an instrument for divine use, so that an entity can communicate or pass messages through you either verbally or by writing.

Charging: Empowering magikal objects with your own energy, such as herbs, crystals or any other tools that are to be used in magik. Compare with Empower.

Circle, magik: This is where all magik and rituals are to be performed, a protective sphere that is created by personal power through the use of magik and governed by the laws of karma.

Clairaudience: To "hear" sound and voices that bring messages from spirits. They can come as a whisper in your ear or a voice inside your mind.

Clairsentience: To "feel," the ability to "sense" spiritual activity rather than seeing or hearing it. Practitioners sense the presence of an entity through heightened emotions.

Clairvoyance: To "see" the spirit world with inner sight. Compare with Psychometry and Scrying.

Cone of power: Energy that is built up within a circle, then later directed to a single goal. In a coven, the energy raised will be as powerful as the members within the group.

Crook and flail: Associated with Osiris, they uphold order and discipline. See Osiris.

Divination: The art of manipulating your conscious mind to awaken the inner power; divining the unknown through the use of meditation, scrying, tarot and other media that involve the use of the psychic mind.

Empower: The process of raising and moving energy into an object, such as a spell or a magik cord, with the aim of increasing its strength.

Energy healing: A technique of healing that involves the channelling of universal energies through your body and onto the client's body. The combination of your own energy and the universal energy that is channelled is a very effective method of healing.

Entity: A foreign intelligence that dwells in another plane of existence. See Spirits.

Ether: The element with which all was created. It is known as the fifth element, the embodiment of spiritual and universal energy.

Evocation: Calling forth an entity to manifest in the astral or on the physical plane. Compare with Invocation.

Folk magic: This involves the use of crystals, herbs, the elements and other natural objects. It is also called natural magik due to its connection with the Earth and combination with your personal power.

Grounding: Shutting down the psychic centres of the body to disperse excess energy that has been built up during the practice of magik or the use of the psychic mind. Sometimes referred to as earthing, as it sends the unwanted energy into the Earth.

Hathor: The Egyptian cow-goddess of all that is feminine. She is the protector of women and a patron of the arts.

Hex craft: The practice of psychic self-defence; includes curses, hexes, potions and incantations, and any other method of protection.

High magik: The term given to the use of "inner senses." It is enforced by your will, so you are able to bring about change through spiritual means. Compare with Low magik.

Horus: The Egyptian hawk-god of prophecy, son of Osiris. He is the lord of art and music, a warrior and the protector of family.

Horus, eye of: This symbolises the facilitation of inner sight and strength; it is used for protection and the enhancement of healing energies. See Third eye.

Invocation: The summoning of an entity within, bringing it into yourself, allowing the entity to speak through your body. It is also used as a way of channelling an entity's power to emerge within you.

Ishtar: The Babylonian creator-goddess; the giver of light, the life force that has sewn the universe together. Keeper of both time and justice, she represents the perfect being.

Isis: The mother-goddess of Egypt, wife of Osiris. She is the mistress of powerful magik and protector of the people.

Ka: The life force of a man; Egyptian for "astral body."

Khat: The body, that which physically dies; Egyptian for "physical shell."

Low magik: The direction of your will by means of spells and rituals to create change on the physical plane. See Magik.

Magik: Known as "heka" in Egyptian, it is the art of moving energy within the spectrum of light in order to bend and control the laws of nature by your own desires, bringing about change to yourself and the environment. From thought to creation, whatever we will it to be, it shall manifest. The thread which holds together all that is, to pull the strings, is working your magik.

Magik, ceremonial: Traditionally used for dedication rituals to the gods, it is a platform for an individual to manipulate objects or their conscious mind in order to achieve the desired results, either by will alone or by spoken words.

Magik, sympathetic: An old form of magik which utilises the power of thought and action. It is visualising or creating a model of the desired outcome before it occurs.

Markta: Meaning "be fortunate your breath," this term reminds us that through absolution only the essence, love, exists. Compare with Ka.

Nature spirits: They are Gnomes (earth), Sylphs (air), Undines (water) and Salamanders (fire). They represent all four elements and combine to form Ether.

Occult: Meaning "hidden," this is the science of metaphysical practice, including psychic phenomena, spirit communication, magik, divination and the study of religion.

Osiris: The father-god and king of Egypt. As the god of the dead, he represents strength and stability, hope and safe passage.

Pentagram: A five-pointed star that symbolises the elements: earth, air, fire, water and Ether. It is used to protect and to harness power. In ritual use, it is inscribed on a circular disk called a pentacle.

Power: The term is associated with the life force that is in everything, an energy which is older than the universe and as unexplainable. It can be harnessed through your own will or by using the power within nature, i.e. crystals and herbs. Compare with Ether.

Psychometry: An extension of clairvoyance meaning to "see" through touch.

Ptah: The Egyptian creator-god known as the architect of the universe.

Pyramid: A symbol of the four elements working together to form a single force. It holds healing properties within its centre and aids in the practice of spiritual growth.

Sakhemet: The Egyptian lion-goddess, the destructive side to the light. As a warrior she defends and protects.

Scrying: Gazing into an object such as a crystal ball, mirror, candle flame or water and receiving visions, images of people and places. See Divination.

Sekhem: Egyptian meaning "life force, human soul."

Silver cord: This is what connects the spirit to the body. Your consciousness can exit your physical shell by way of dreams and astral travel with no threat of separation.

Skyclad: A term commonly used in Wicca and some other magikal practices meaning naked, referring to the performance of ritual without clothing.

Spell: Magik that combines the power of spoken words with the use of potions and ingredients. It is a dramatisation of the means used to bring about the end; the means are the components relating to the mechanics behind manifestation, and the end is the focus of your intent, spell-t out.

Spirits: Astral beings that are with us all throughout life. They are here to guide, teach and help us grow spiritually and mentally. Variously known as angels, fairies and guardians, they dwell within the light and bring their gift of unconditional love.

Talisman: An object that carries special properties, that is charged with energy and gives the bearer power over another force. They are created to ward off evil, protect, heal and, in some cases, open doors to hidden powers of the mind. Also known as amulets or seals.

Temple: A sacred place where Wiccan rituals, circles and magik are performed.

Third eye: This is located above the eyebrows, below the centre of the forehead. It is the psychic centre of the body.

Thoth: The Egyptian ibis-god, god of truth and wisdom, lord of Akasha and scribe to the gods.

Trance: A deliberate act of departure from the conscious mind by lowering brainwave activity and relaxing the body into an altered state. A lesser form is known as meditation, in which you reach a state of serenity.

Triple Goddess: The three faces of the Goddess: Maiden, Mother and Crone.

Wennefer: The name of Osiris.

West, the: This refers to what are known as the summer lands, the place where the dead dwell. In Egyptian the dead are also referred to as those of the west or westerners.

Wicca: A modern religion that is associated with witchcraft; its origins date back before organised religion. It combines the principles and ideals of the old faith with a modern outlook; all that has changed is the evolution of magik and belief that have come from being the children of the God and Goddess.

Widdershins: Meaning "backwards," in Wicca it refers to the performance of a particular ritual counter-clockwise.

New Releases… also from Sid Harta Publishers

OTHER BEST SELLING SID HARTA TITLES CAN BE FOUND AT
http://sidharta.com.au   http://Anzac.sidharta.com
※※※

HAVE YOU WRITTEN A STORY?
http://publisher-guidelines.com
※※

DID YOU KNOW YOU CAN FOLLOW US ONLINE? THE AUTHOR CAN BE FOUND AT
https://www.facebook.com/EtheanSouleRainbowMedium/

New Releases... also from Sid Harta Publishers

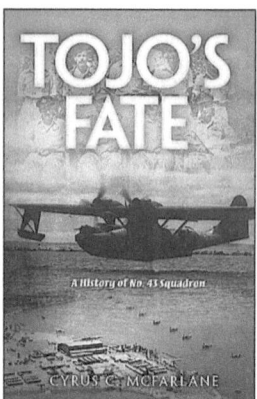

OTHER BEST SELLING SID HARTA TITLES CAN BE FOUND AT
http://sidharta.com.au   http://Anzac.sidharta.com

HAVE YOU WRITTEN A STORY?
http://publisher-guidelines.com

DID YOU KNOW YOU CAN FOLLOW US ONLINE? THE AUTHOR CAN BE FOUND AT
https://www.facebook.com/EtheanSouleRainbowMedium/

Best-selling titles by Kerry B. Collison

Readers are invited to visit our publishing websites at:
http://sidharta.com.au
http://publisher-guidelines.com/

Kerry B. Collison's home pages:
http://www.authorsden.com/visit/author.asp?AuthorID=2239
http://www.expat.or.id/sponsors/collison.html
email: author@sidharta.com.au

Purchase Sid Harta titles online at:
http://sidharta.com.au

Want to know more? Readers are encouraged to follow the Author online:
https://www.facebook.com/EtheanSouleRainbowMedium/
https://www.facebook.com/UnfoldingMagik/

New Releases… also from Sid Harta Publishers

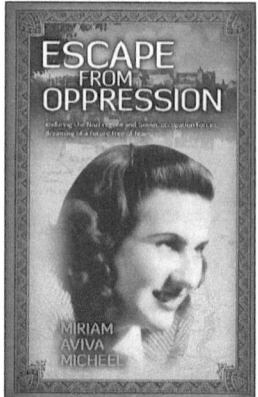

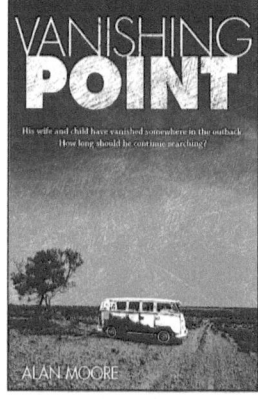

OTHER BEST SELLING SID HARTA TITLES CAN BE FOUND AT
http://sidharta.com.au   http://Anzac.sidharta.com
***

HAVE YOU WRITTEN A STORY?
http://publisher-guidelines.com
**

DID YOU KNOW YOU CAN FOLLOW US ONLINE? THE AUTHOR CAN BE FOUND AT
https://www.facebook.com/EtheanSouleRainbowMedium/

www.ingramcontent.com/pod-product-compliance
Lightning Source LLC
Chambersburg PA
CBHW030136170426
43199CB00008B/85